GOOD TEACHERS, GOOD SCHOOLS

'Good schools think *with* people and not *to* people', argues David Hudson in this thought-provoking practical guide for those wanting to bridge the gap between middle and senior management roles and make a difference in their schools. Accessibly and engagingly written and packed with real-life examples, this book will prove essential reading for ambitious teachers and deputy heads everywhere. While many management books tend to overcomplicate, David writes with refreshing clarity and simplicity of thought. He sets out to inspire his readers to improve their practice and offers tried-and-tested strategies and solutions.

   Good Teachers, Good Schools is a must-have read for anyone interested in a senior school leadership role and for those leaders keen to improve their leadership style. The book covers every aspect of school leadership, from the decisions senior school leaders need to make – such as running meetings, staffing and communication with staff and pupils – to the difference between management and leadership, and on to curriculum involvement including monitoring evaluation and self-evaluation. David Hudson encapsulates many principles that have made him a successful school leader.

David Hudson has been teaching in secondary schools since 1973 and he has had a wide range of leadership and management roles including that of head teacher in two 11–18 schools.

GOOD TEACHERS, GOOD SCHOOLS

HOW TO CREATE A SUCCESSFUL SCHOOL

David Hudson

Routledge
Taylor & Francis Group

LONDON AND NEW YORK

First published 2009
by Routledge
2 Park Square, Milton Park, Abingdon, Oxon OX14 4RN

Simultaneously published in the USA and Canada
by Routledge
270 Madison Avenue, New York, NY 10016

Routledge is an imprint of the Taylor & Francis Group, an informa business

© 2009 David Hudson

Typeset in Aldus Roman and Scala Sans by
Florence Production Ltd, Stoodleigh, Devon
Printed and bound in Great Britain by
CPI Antony Rowe, Chippenham, Wiltshire

British Library Cataloguing in Publication Data
A catalogue record for this book is available from the British Library

Library of Congress Cataloging in Publication Data
Hudson, David, 1951–
  Good teachers, good schools: how you can create a successful
  school / David Hudson.
      p. cm.
  Includes bibliographical references.
  1. Educational leadership – Great Britain. 2. School management
and organisation – Great Britain. 3. Education, Secondary – Great
Britain – Administration. I. Title.
  LB2900.5.H83 2008
  371.200941 – dc22   2008013909

ISBN10: 0–415–47132–X (pbk)

ISBN13: 978–0–415–47132–9 (pbk)

CONTENTS

ACKNOWLEDGEMENTS

I am very grateful to Jenny and Abigail Hudson and Sharon Bailey who proofread the book and worked to my imposed deadlines despite their very busy schedules and lives.

Elaine Renavent and Sharon Bailey helped a great deal with the sections on data analysis and monitoring, evaluation and review; Tim Delight with the information about pastoral monitoring evaluation and review; and Dean Jones on examination technique – I am extremely grateful to all four colleagues and am fortunate to be working with them day to day.

Wyll Willis – now a head teacher himself – was the inspiration behind the ideas on boys' achievement.

INTRODUCTION

Most teachers and parents, particularly in secondary schools, are extremely pleased when students show an interest in their own learning. Most teachers are also ready to assist parents to play an active part in their child's education and schooling. This is particularly true of teachers who are themselves, or have recently been, parents of teenagers. So why is day-to-day, detailed parental involvement uncommon in primary schools (despite what many might think) and extremely rare in the secondary school context?

Teachers want parents to be more involved; parents want to be more involved and yet they, the parents, are less and less drawn in as their child gets older.

It is hard to escape the conclusion, not only that the knowledge, understanding and skills necessary for parents to be as fully involved as they would like become more sophisticated as the child grows – the reason often given – but also that the student increasingly defines their necessary and unavoidable role of 'go-between' as that of 'gate keeper'.

Parents need to be informed if they are to know what questions to ask and if they are to have a route to influence their child's education, but this presupposes that their child *wants* mum or dad to have influence. It is the duty of the school to provide that information and to facilitate that route, but a prerequisite to achieving this is the realisation that all schools, and particularly secondary schools, have an unauthorised and unsanctioned Quality Assurance procedure taking place; and the 'Head of QA' is the student. Children who do not want their parents to get to know are ideally placed to get their wish.

One cannot expect and would not want non-professionals to have to become quasi educators to fulfil their role. However, increased and better informed involvement of parents is a major factor for good schooling and the days when mum and dad were expected, indeed 'required' to turn up looking interested and supportive and then leave, are long gone.

This book is designed to inform and to stimulate discussion and debate among and between teachers and school senior leaders and it provides good advice and tried and tested strategies for the reader to put into practice should they so wish. It is also written in such a way as to enable and facilitate the role of parents, governors and Local Education Authority (LEA) personnel.

Teachers who read it will find much that is new and they will confirm and consolidate what they already know. In addition, they will find a renewed clarity and reasons and explanations for the day-to-day experiences and challenges in their work with adolescents. The book is unashamedly practical and is written by someone who still knows what it is like to teach Year 9 bottom set on a wet and windy Friday afternoon after they have had PE!

The newly qualified teacher (NQT) or student on a course to become a teacher will, probably for the first time, feel the luxury of proactive thinking as they read the book. The NQT is constantly accosted by needy children, all of whom seem to understand the system better than they do, and it is in this environment that they have to learn their trade – a crib sheet is no bad thing.

School senior leaders will find a good deal that is fresh and innovative and, most importantly, they will notice a coherence in this book that will enable them to define and refine their core goals and purpose and, most importantly, to communicate their vision to all sectors within their school.

Middle leaders who aspire to senior leadership will find the book stimulating and thought provoking. This group of teachers has experience of the process of decision making but their experience of decision taking is limited by the hierarchical nature of our schools. Therefore, they, more than any others, have a drive and need to formulate their individual vision and, more specifically, the non-negotiable concepts and goals that will ultimately define them and their school.

Their personal educational philosophy and value system will already exist; but the step to senior leadership will only be taken successfully by those that have clearly and thoroughly defined the processes and practices that they can and will employ when *they* become the lead decision taker.

All professionals working in schools will recognise *their* school in the pages of this book and they will see immediately a use and context for what they read. The inherent 'transference' problems that we have all faced on courses – 'that's a fantastic idea, now how do I exploit it back at the ranch?' – or in lessons – 'they can only do graphs in maths lessons; science is different' – are deliberately avoided. Entertaining and even informing are not enough and this book will only be successful if it affects and improves actual classroom experience for the teacher and for the student.

I hope that some parents might read it and those that do will be able to bring their unique knowledge and understanding of their own child to discussions with teachers; they will be able to offer insights and advice that can only help and inform the whole process.

Governors and LEA personnel who read the book will find their role of critical friend more 'do-able' and they will be more able to provide practical help and assistance.

The school/home/student triangle remains a major untapped pathway to success and a book that attempts to link the three sides by not overtly distinguishing between them has to be at the very least, a step in the right direction.

In order to enable *any* interested adult and even any student to be sufficiently informed to become as involved with the work of their school as they would wish, I have, where possible and appropriate, assumed no prior knowledge. Indeed, there is a section immediately following this introduction that outlines the nuts and bolts of all of our schools.

Senior leaders and experienced teachers might decide to skip this section; parents, inexperienced, newly qualified and prospective teachers will read it with interest. I suspect that several teachers (even those that have been in the business for many years) and school support staff will find this section clarifies much that is regularly talked about, but that they have never been able or prepared to admit they have never really understood.

1

SCHOOL SYSTEMS AND STRUCTURES

SECONDARY SCHOOL

All schools are different but secondary schools often have operating systems and structures that are similar or, to the non-professional eye, identical.

All have a senior leadership (sometimes called management) team that typically consists of the head teacher, one or two deputy head teachers and two to four assistant head teachers. One of the deputy heads is named first deputy head teacher so that there is clarity about who takes over if the head teacher is ill or indisposed for any length of time.

These senior leadership team (SLT) members will tend to lead on: curriculum, finance, staff development, student development (often called 'pastoral'), data analysis (sometimes referred to as raising student attainment) and, in many schools, learning.

Working under the SLT will be the middle leaders or managers. In many of the larger secondary schools there are seven or so 'senior' middle leaders, often known as faculty leaders, and within each faculty there will be several departments each with its own head.

Some faculties are easily identified, and all schools that have faculties will have faculty leaders for mathematics, English and science. PE or Sport is also easy to separate. The departments of history, geography and religious studies are often grouped in the

Humanities faculty and art, music and drama often become Expressive Arts.

Subjects such as design technology: resistant materials (wood, metal, plastic); food (used to be called home economics and, way back in time, domestic science); graphics (all about product design); possibly electronics; and ICT (information communication technology – computer study) – might be in a stand-alone Technology faculty but are sometimes attached to one of the other faculties. Dance might come under the PE/Sport umbrella or the Expressive Arts faculty. Modern Foreign Languages is usually a separate faculty but can sometimes be grouped with English to become the Communications faculty. Subjects such as personal social and health education (PSHE), citizenship, business studies and economics, sociology and psychology are usually grouped with Humanities; media studies with English; and child care and health and social care with Science.

The faculties at my school are: English, Mathematics, Science, Expressive Arts and Technology, Modern Foreign Languages, Humanities (includes ICT) and Sport.

Having no more than eight faculties enables senior leaders to meet and discuss with a small group of key subject-based professionals who, between them, cover the whole school. Larger groups tend to provide a platform for some to make speeches while others listen, so profitable debate in groups of more than 10 is rare.

The pastoral deputy head (or assistant head) will usually lead five heads of year, one assigned to each year group and often, particularly in big schools, there will also be a leader for each Key Stage. The KS3 (Years 7, 8 and 9, 11–14-year-olds) leader is sometimes called head of lower school; KS4 (Years 10 and 11, 14–16-year-olds) – head of upper school; and, in an 11–18 school, KS5 (Years 12 and 13, 17- and 18-year-olds) – head of sixth form. A big sixth form will also have a head of Year 12 and head of Year 13.

Each year group will contain a number of tutor groups or forms each with its own tutor or form teacher. These are mixed-ability groups that take into account both friendships to be encouraged, and also liaisons that parents recommend should be avoided at all costs. Schools try to limit the number of students in these tutor groups to 25, so 300 students in a year group becomes 12 tutor groups with 12 tutors, and the school is said to be 12 Form Entry or 12 FE.

The tutor will register the students twice daily – morning session and an afternoon session; this is a legal requirement. All children have to attend for a maximum of 190 school days in any one year – 380 possible attendance marks. The teachers will attend for 195 days and these five 'extra' days are used for teacher training or INSET (In Service Training) while the students are absent.

Registering students is very important, but the main job of a tutor is much more central to the business of the school. The head teacher is *in loco parentis* while the student is in school but, in practice, this duty falls to the teachers and, in particular, the tutor of that student. The tutor will thus be expected to know more than any other member of staff about each student in their tutor group and the student will often develop a very strong bond with their tutor. The tutor is the nearest thing to a school-based parent.

The role of tutor is undertaken by full-time teachers as an everyday requirement; it is not regarded as extra to a teacher's substantive role. Some teachers will, however, apply for, and be awarded, a management or leadership role in addition to their teaching commitment and role as a tutor. This is additional to their main contract and there will be a payment attached to this extra responsibility. This payment is known as a teaching and learning responsibility or a TLR.

TLRs function via a hierarchical ladder where TLR 2 is 'below' TLR 1. The 'ranking' in order of increasing pay is therefore as follows:

Level 2
    TLR 2a   over £2,000 per annum extra salary
    TLR 2b   approx. £4,000 per annum extra salary
    TLR 2c   approx. £6,000 per annum extra salary

Level 1
    TLR 1b   over £8,000 per annum extra salary
    TLR 1d   over £11,000 per annum extra salary

Clearly the greater the level of responsibility, the greater the requirement to lead on behalf of the school, the more money is paid.

The move from TLR 2 to TLR 1 is determined by the number of full-time staff (full-time equivalents or FTEs) that the TLR post holder manages or leads.

In addition to money, secondary school teachers with 'extra' responsibility get extra non-contact time (free periods) over and above the normal allocation for that school. A school with a six, 50-minute-period day (30-period week), would normally allocate five non-contact periods to a teacher with no additional responsibility. These five periods can be, but usually are not, called upon to cover a lesson where another teacher is absent – schools can require teachers to do this 38 times in an academic year. One of the weekly non-contact periods is a protected non-contact time so that the teacher can plan to use it with no expectation of being 'on call'. A faculty leader would typically have seven non-contacts, head of department – six, head of year – seven, etc.

Increasingly schools are employing classroom supervisors to 'cover' for absent teachers. These are normally not qualified teachers and they are not normally expected to teach the class. Instead, they 'manage' the class and ensure that the work set by the absent teacher or by the head of department or faculty leader is completed properly.

In addition, secondary schools will have many teaching assistants (TAs) – sometimes called non-teaching assistants (NTAs). These adults are also not qualified teachers but the TAs are deployed in classes to work alongside the teacher – often, but not exclusively, the class will contain students that have a special educational need (SEN), and the TA will work class-wide or exclusively with a particular student. Some students might have an official 'Statement' of specific need and this might involve a certain number of hours of 'one-to-one' help for that student.

Schools will also have learning mentors who will review work done and progress made with individual students. Learning mentors, TAs and classroom supervisors are all 'unqualified' and are referred to as 'support staff' but they play an increasingly vital and central role in schools.

Qualified teachers start their careers on the main scale of payments (M1 to M6), and each year they move to the next point on the scale – this is payment for experience, and while it can be 'blocked' by head teachers, it rarely is. In their first year these teachers are referred to as NQTs and they have to successfully complete this probationary one-year period. Should the head teacher refuse to authorise and document their successful completion of this first year in the profession, the teacher cannot continue and cannot, from that point on, become a qualified teacher in any school – again, this is very rare.

Unless they are recipients of a TLR, teachers will reach the top of main scale after six years and then they can apply for 'threshold'. This is the performance related route from main scale to the upper pay spine of payment, and it is at the discretion of the head teacher. Threshold pay is approximately £2,000 per year, and once they have successfully negotiated threshold, teachers can apply every two or so years, to move to the next point on the upper pay spine. There are three points on the upper pay spine.

The two years minimum period before an application is made is because the head teacher is required to 'judge' their perform-ance against the work of, at least, their last two years. Should the teacher have moved schools during that two-year period, their present head teacher should contact their previous head teacher before making a decision.

Main scale, threshold and the upper pay spine are all awarded for being a good or very good classroom teacher, not for responsibility and work outside of the classroom. The key performance indicator is the academic progress of the students that that teacher has taught. The head teacher will monitor this closely before sanctioning a performance-related pay rise.

Those teachers that also aspire to management and leader-ship outside of the classroom will move via the TLR 2s and TLR 1s ladders to what is known as the leadership spine of payment. Senior leaders such as head teachers, deputy head teachers and assistant head teachers are paid on this. The particular grade or level a senior leader occupies on this scale of payment depends on the size of the school in which the senior leader works.

PRIMARY SCHOOL

The systems and structures that typically exist in primary schools are much more similar to those that exist in secondary schools than one would imagine.

Three- to four-year-olds are 'pre-school' and four- to five-year-olds are 'primary/infant' and are described as 'reception'. Three- to five-year-olds are at the early years/foundation stage. Five- to seven-year-olds are Key Stage 1 (primary/infant) with five- to six-year-olds being Year 1 and six- to seven-year-olds Year 2. There is a Key Stage 1 (SATs) test in maths and English based mainly on teacher assessment. Key Stage 2 is seven- to eleven-year-olds (primary/junior) with Key Stage 2 (SATs) tests in maths, English and science.

The school is almost always much smaller than the typical secondary school and eight teaching staff are going to generate far fewer TLRs than, for example, 80 staff. There is always a head, usually a deputy and then one or two TLRs to lead on a section of the school or a pedagogic area.

Lessons are usually taught around extended projects and each 50 minutes or so may not have a discrete learning objective in the way that it would have in a secondary school. The literacy and maths hours still operate but less rigidly – though government prescription is still present and, I think it is fair to say, is resisted by primary school teachers far more than their secondary counterparts. Testing in the quantified/snapshot-in-time way is anathema to most primary school teachers.

Each class in primary school will be mixed ability and it will consist of students of similar age; it will be taught and registered by one teacher. There may be a few teaching assistants and possibly one learning mentor, but it is unlikely that there will be cover supervisors to step in when a teacher is away. The head teacher is often 'non-teaching'.

Clearly, primary schools *begin* the formal learning process for all children and they would not expect all entrants to be 'the finished article'. However, it is crucial that the primary school is not starting from absolute zero when a child first presents, and certain skills are essential. Such skills are being able to:

- dress and undress themselves;
- use a pen and pencil and a pair of scissors;
- use a knife and fork;
- say and write their name;
- use the toilet independently;
- count to 10;
- play with other children and share;
- respond to simple instructions.

It is, perhaps, surprising how many children at four or five years old cannot do this and some attend school still unable to talk properly and some even in nappies.

Secondary and many primary school teachers may well not realise the significance of this. However, I am absolutely certain that the five-year-old that arrives in school without these basic skills, inevitably becomes the eight-year-old that is learning far less than they should and is already lagging behind their peers. This student is usually already all too aware of their deficiencies and well on the way to becoming the 14-year-old disruptive who has long since lost her/his stakeholder characteristics and who cannot wait to leave full-time education.

The tanker begins its journey at three; to focus on the need to set it off correctly is so much more sensible than trying to stop it and turn it around once it has reached full speed.

2

GOVERNORS, GOVERNANCE AND OFSTED

Governor

One who governs; one invested with supreme authority; chief administrator of an institution; member of a committee responsible for an organisation or institution.

Collins English Dictionary

Governing bodies were invented over 130 years ago, and few of us would claim that today's schools are even remotely reminiscent of those Bob Cratchet institutions of the 1870s, where the head teacher had to seek permission from 'The School Board' to put an extra lump of coal on the classroom fire.

LEAs, now often called LAs – for some obscure reason the word 'education' is deemed no longer necessary – also have a governance role, in that they have 'responsibility' for the group of schools geographically grouped under the umbrella of the council they serve. LEAs have responsibility, but the 'power' lies in the schools, with the governing body and, in particular, with the head teacher.

As it has always been, today's schools and school leaders need an LEA, and particularly a governing body, that is a:

- trusted and well informed critical friend;
- mechanism and system for accountability that is regular and

on-going, and which informs and improves practice as well as measuring it;

- forum for 'strategic' discussion and thinking.

The overwhelming majority of governing bodies and LEAs are trusted by senior leaders, and by the teachers and support staff in our schools. However, in practice it is difficult for either to become truly involved in the day-to-day running, or the strategic thinking and planning of our schools.

Governors tend to be lay people (not professionally involved in education – usually parents), and LEAs tend to be professionals, who have often never taught in schools, or who taught briefly many years ago. So a great deal of school time and effort is spent ensuring that both governors and LEAs are well informed.

All head teachers produce three to six written reports per academic year to service the three to six full governing body (around 19 governors for a large secondary school) meetings. They also provide information, and attend governors' sub-committee meetings on: curriculum, finance and staffing and premises – probably another six meetings per academic year. These meetings are, on average, two or three hours in duration. The focus of the reports occasionally overlaps, but is seldom identical. School governors and LEA personnel try to get into school during school time, but work commitments make these visits infrequent.

School improvement visits between the school's SIP (School Improvement Partner) who is sometimes (50 per cent of the time) a professional with head teacher experience (one in two SIPs are LEA personnel who have little teaching, let alone head teacher experience), and the head teacher of the school, take place around three to six times per year and are often followed by a written report.

Schools and governors produce a School Development Plan (one year and three year), and this is discussed at governing body meetings and with the SIP throughout the academic year. Departments and faculties in secondary schools also produce development plans which are monitored and evaluated by the school's senior leaders.

Increasingly, and quite rightly, the accent is on self-review and Ofsted (government inspection service) expects schools to continually update their SEF (self-evaluation form). This has to be available to Ofsted on-line at all times and senior leaders must therefore keep it up to date and 'current'.

Ofsted now give schools just two days' notice of their arrival for an inspection, and they are in the school for about two days. They then categorise the school as: 'outstanding', 'good', 'satisfactory', or 'inadequate', and when they are 'inadequate' schools can be given 'notice to improve', or they can be put into 'special measures'. Schools that are categorised as inadequate will be expected to show significant improvement within one year, and can be closed down if they fail to improve, or do not improve sufficiently or quickly enough.

The separate categories inspectors look for during an inspection are:

- overall effectiveness of the school;
- achievement and standards;
- personal development and well-being;
- quality of provision;
- leadership and management.

Each element is graded with one of the four grades mentioned above and then the school is put into an overall category.

Clearly, parents, more than any other group of adults, have a vested interest in their school doing well, and since governing bodies are mainly made up of parents, the parent voice is safeguarded to some extent.

However, many parents don't want to be governors, and they prefer to join the Parent Teachers' Association (PTA) or the Home School Association. Rightly or wrongly, these have become a vehicle to raise money for the school and they don't actually provide many real opportunities for parents to get involved in the life of the school.

Despite all comment to the contrary, raising funding is not a particularly necessary activity these days, and parents are misled into thinking that once their efforts have raised a few pounds, and this money has found its way into school funds, that they 'have done their bit' for the education of their children.

This apparently inclusive activity of PTA Committee membership is thus in reality exclusive since it defines the activities that parents are allowed to become involved in and, by definition, the activities that they are not. We should not be surprised that few secondary schools these days have vibrant and dynamic PTAs.

3

LEADERSHIP

So, schools are hierarchical, with 'leaders' paid most and at the top.

WHAT DOES LEADERSHIP LOOK LIKE?

There are those who would define a leader as someone who has an 'authority' word in their job title. In schools these roles would be: head of department or subject, head of year, director of sixth form, member of the SLT, head teacher, deputy head teacher, etc.

In reality, the need and requirement to lead exists for every adult who works with children. Indeed, this obligation is, arguably, more clear-cut and definitive than in any other profession or job.

Students operate through groups and every group of people will have a dominant character or several dominant personalities and in every classroom there will always be at least one leader; the person that at any given moment will decide the agenda, define the parameters, set the tone and drive the pace. If this is not an adult who cares deeply about the success of the organisation and the individuals in that organisation, then the business of learning in that classroom, and beyond that throughout the school, is in deep trouble.

There is no doubt that everybody has the capacity to lead given the right situation. However, those we might categorise as 'leaders' not only have the necessary attributes and the confidence to use them, they also have a certain mind-set that encourages them to grasp the reins in most situations. They tend to stand out from the crowd. They're the person you don't always like, but you do tend to remember.

> **So leaders 'are', they don't 'aspire to be'.**
> **They don't 'go on leadership courses to learn how to do it', they just 'are'.**

Are *you* a leader? Give yourself an 'always', 'sometimes' or 'never' rating for the questions shown on pages 18–19.

So, how did you score and does it matter?

Clearly it only matters if you are in the position of leader and do not possess the qualities required to lead. Or if you possess those qualities but are leading in an environment about which you know nothing.

In my view, school leaders who are poor leaders in the classroom – in other words they are mediocre or poor teachers – fail this 'about which you know nothing' criterion. These people are seemingly unaware that the primary purpose of a school is student learning. They don't look for learning, which is probably neither here nor there since they wouldn't recognise it if they did!

These leaders, therefore, find it very difficult to define where the class, year group, department, faculty or organisation is, in terms of progress. They find it impossible to play a lead in producing one- and three-year plans full of strategies to get the students and the school to where they need to be. Most worrying is that they don't know what they don't know.

THE DIFFERENCE BETWEEN MANAGEMENT AND LEADERSHIP

The dictionary defines the word **manage** as: 'To be in charge of, succeed in doing, control, handle.' Synonyms for **lead** are: guide, conduct, persuade, direct. 'Manage' implies a 'hands on' involvement with the process and 'lead' suggests a detachment and delegation.

ARE YOU A LEADER?

1 Are you determined in virtually all situations to be yourself?

Good leaders often find it almost impossible to be anyone or anything but themselves. They exude consistency even when they are wrong and, while leaders come in all shapes and sizes, those being led always know what to expect.

2 Are you a good communicator?

This is as much about listening as talking and good communicators are intuitively aware of the impact of their words and gestures. They are clear and unambiguous.

3 Are you prepared to fight for what you believe is right?

People who have no opinions of their own; who can't or won't do it themselves; and who have no values that they will defend no matter what the opposition, tend to be very vocal: 'I don't vote, they're all the same, what's the point?'; 'Schools today are terrible. In the good old days everybody could at least read, write and add up.'

These professional critics know beyond all doubt that those people who do fight for what they believe is a good cause, and who are genuinely trying to make a difference, are wrong.

Therefore all leaders can expect criticism (almost always from the sidelines and ill-informed). This criticism is, I'm afraid, continuous – it comes with the territory. Leadership is not a popularity contest.

4 Do you set a good example?

A leader who says one thing and does another is dead in the water. Stories will be told about the leader and many will be untrue. However, the overall and perceived image of the leader needs to enhance her/his leadership. Good leaders are constantly in tune with the voters.

5 Do you understand the need to create a high challenge/low fear environment?

It is all about results and outcomes. The people being led want to feel that all that hard work has paid off. As such, they expect to be challenged and held to account. When this is stretching but realistic, and the accountability is exercised by someone who is overtly supportive, then it is effective and it will bring about improvement.

We all learn and progress by making mistakes and we all, adults and children alike, need to feel that it is all right to 'have a go', especially when we are unsure and when there is a risk of failing.

6 Do you understand the need to use the finances and resources of the organisation wisely and well?

Good leaders of organisations commanding a budget know the difference between 'value' and 'cost', but they also have their finger on the financial pulse of the organisation at all times.

Inevitably some of the funding is 'spoken for'; the good leader knows what isn't and then makes sure that this money is used and used wisely and to good effect – saving for a rainy day is not an option in this increasingly fast and ever changing world.

7 Do you care and does your team know that you care?

This should be axiomatic for the good leader, but leadership is a lonely business and it is very easy to be self-contained and apparently aloof; when a leader feels passionate about something, the people being led need to see that passion.

There is no doubting that the two processes and skills are very similar, but leaders are not managers and a lack of understanding of the difference between the two will be to the profound detriment of the school.

Schools, like many business organisations, tend to have plenty of managers and very few leaders; regrettably it is much easier for a leader to behave like a manager than it is for a manager to perform the leadership role. An example of this is the senior 'leader' who claims proudly that they 'manage by walking about' because the troops need to 'see them working hard and doing their bit'. This person does lots of cover lessons and is always 'on duty'; they organise official chats with staff the only purpose of which is to show them that they 'care'. Undoubtedly, they work very hard, if not very effectively, but what they are doing cannot and should not be categorised as leading.

The drive of this person is perhaps understandable even though it is not acceptable. Leaders are isolated and they are often open to the criticisms of the under-informed and over-opinionated – 'all the real work is being done by us poor bloody infantry!' Leaders have to be mentally resilient; those that have a need to be 'liked' are in the wrong job.

The teacher in the classroom who doesn't take charge and cause the students to work hard and fulfil their (the students') responsibilities and who puts having a good relationship with the students before student learning is operating in the same unacceptable way. Effective classrooms are all about learning, they are not about teaching and the teacher who focuses on him/herself has the wrong focus.

Good leaders clearly understand the difference between thinking and behaving strategically and thinking and behaving operationally. They are skilled in time management and they understand that their role must be strategic if their hard work is to be effective; they can and do exploit the 'helicopter factor'.

This is a technique that enables them to rise above the particulars of a situation (as if in a helicopter) and perceive it 'in context'. Those leaders who constantly utilise this technique are able to take on board – where appropriate and necessary – both the specific and the holistic. They are much more effective as a result.

If we imagine the 'details' as being the separate pieces of a jigsaw puzzle, good leaders have at the forefront of their minds at all times what the picture on the box of the jigsaw should look like. They continually look for different and more interesting ways to describe this picture to all involved. They have the capacity to constantly rise up to the necessary height to be able to check the box properly, before drifting down to examine with great care the complex angles and textures of each individual piece.

Too many leaders are either constantly flying high, and are consequently nonplussed when, like a speck in a never ending sky, they are imperceptible to those working on terra firma; or, they are working very hard to be seen to be hovering low (managing by walking about; being popular), so low that their view is terminally blurred and they may as well land and save the cost of the aviation fuel.

MANAGING CHANGE

Good teachers are aware that managing change is what they do every minute of every day in their classroom.

The learning objectives of each lesson are, by definition, unknown territory to the students; they represent transform-ation and movement when the audience longs for stability and familiarity. It is not a 'safe' environment in that sense, and student (particularly the teenager) fear and apprehension will be ready to break through and take control at any moment. Changing environments are never comfortable, but in skilled hands they can be exciting and even thrilling.

I regret that there are many in education who would accept much of what I say above as necessary and good 'for children in the classroom', but would reject it all when applied to adults and to the schools in which the adults work. These people regard the need for *them* to change as 'rare' and they tend to point to: 'initiative fatigue', 'work/life balance', 'increased bureaucracy' and, perversely, 'falling standards' as reasons to maintain the status quo. They say that managing change is a concept that only needs to be addressed, and therefore understood, when, and if, change is necessary. For them, change is avoidable.

To cling to a comfort zone is, perhaps, natural and a desire to explore the unknown is arguably not 'the norm'. However, anyone who believes that this twenty-first-century society of ours is not constantly and dramatically changing and is not changing at a pace that is as frenetic as it ever has been in the whole of human history, is living in a different world to mine. To expect a school to operate separately from, and outside, that change culture and still to manage to be a 'good' school is to be at best naive and, more likely, negligent.

High expectation requires a determination and drive to strive to do better tomorrow no matter how well we have done today. It requires a clear mind-set that there is no standing still; we either go forward or we go back.

Constant change in the classroom and in the school is therefore a forerunner to success. Change is, and will continue to be, our ever present companion and it needs to be relentlessly and consistently 'managed' and led.

Michael Fullan's recipe for the **management of change** is:

- break the required change into phases or modules;
- establish an implementation plan which should be brief and not too elaborate;
- seek to reduce early costs and to increase early rewards;
- stress on-going training;
- focus on the support that is available;
- maintain support but also maintain pressure (deadlines, etc.).

(Fullan 1985)

Good teachers and good managers of change should not therefore plan the change so thoroughly that it is months before anything actually happens. A clear and distinct objective with clear and precise success criteria should not take long – two or three weeks – and since change should be seen as a process not an event this is perfectly acceptable, even advisable.

It is probably a clear and perceptible advantage for the leader's plan to be less than 100 per cent accurate prior to implementation. Students aren't the only ones who learn by making mistakes and it is no bad thing for adults not to 'get it right' first time. The pace and momentum of change is much more important than a desire for perfection.

Students get one crack at compulsory education. They are in Year 5 or Year 8 just once and that 'year' lasts for just 38 weeks. The sense of urgency is palpable and, while teachers, and particularly leaders and managers, will be expected to 'get it right', they will be equally required to 'get on with it! – a hypothetical interview candidate who not only displays impatience to immediately improve upon the status quo, but also shows a determination to carry out step change (one leap rather than a steady drip), should be appointed without vacillation.

Senior leaders and senior managers who believe and engage in step change are atypical. These people are calculated risk takers and they have such a clear vision and philosophy that they understand the need to take these calculated risks to achieve their very succinct and precise goals. These leaders will, for example, put budgetary considerations to one side and buy 200 computers instead of 20 – because ICT is central to the fortunes of a twenty-first-century school, and the students already in the school, need the computers *now*.

To implement step change requires a clear moral purpose. To continue undaunted when eyebrows are raised even when things don't altogether go according to plan, and to resist the temptation to play safe when the inevitable doubts begin to nag, requires integrity and, yes, bravery.

Risk takers in education don't do it for the buzz, or to be 'on the edge'. They do it because they are not prepared to settle for any less for other people's children than they would expect for their own and thus the 'details' are immaterial, as long as the fundamentals are achieved.

WHAT GOOD SCHOOLS LOOK LIKE

A school, like any large organisation, operates through a web of interacting teams. The development of the individual within a team context is a key factor. Human or personal needs must come first – the human perspective is the starting point.

If all team members genuinely feel that they are developing and learning under the guidance of a good mentor, then their personal contribution and commitment will increase.

The leader's viewpoint is a privileged one. This is particularly true for teachers in the classroom and for senior leaders – especially head teachers – in the whole school situation. Those leaders who are aware of, and who accept, this fact, will use their unique freedom to act decisively in order to restore balance, or to satisfy the needs of particular team members. Fine judgement, a sense of timing, and an ability to retrospectively explore what has taken place, are all leadership traits.

Good leaders in schools need to know and understand how to manage change, but also, and most importantly, what 'good' schools look like.

A 'GOOD' SCHOOL

A 'good' school is one that:

- is collaborative;
- is pupil centred;

- has a commitment to a variety of teaching and learning styles with as much student involvement in their own learning process as possible;
- has explicit high expectations;
- has shared values and goals;
- provides an effective learning environment;
- emphasises the value of positive reinforcement;
- is, itself, always learning;
- affords students rights and responsibilities where all involved are left in no doubt that disrupting the education of other students is totally unacceptable;
- has good and mutually beneficial links with the business community;
- has strong and valued home–school links.

This last point is still a major issue for all schools but for secondary schools in particular; it should be remembered that in most of our schools children spend just 25 hours per week 'being taught'. Clearly, therefore, the need for good home–school links is indisputable.

Tizard and Hughes in their 1984 book, *Young Children Learning, Talking and Thinking at Home and at School*, found that: 'The home provides a very powerful learning environment.'

They listed five reasons:

1 The range of activities in the home is greater than in the school.
2 The shared common life helps the parent to 'make sense' of experiences.
3 The smaller number of children leads to a greater share of adult life.
4 The home learning experiences are in contexts of greater significance to the child. Schools have artificial devices to try to mimic these.
5 The parental relationship is close and often intense. Parents have definite expectations and they will pursue them with whatever energy they have available. This unease converts potential advantage into actual advantage.

However, despite the often-stated desire to improve and develop strong home–school links in our secondary schools, we still have a sudden drop in parental involvement at student age 11, with no satisfactory explanation for it.

Schools must address the very real need to understand and to build upon home-learning. Parental involvement comes in a complete – all or nothing – package and schools must choose the whole deal or content themselves with what is, in effect, no deal at all. Keeping parents informed about the learning taking place at school and about what they, the parent, can do to enhance and improve it, is essential.

THE DECISIONS SCHOOL SENIOR LEADERS NEED TO TAKE AND WHY

Good and very good head teachers and senior leaders, have a very clearly defined value system and philosophy for education, but just as importantly, and more particular to them, they also have action-based imperatives – in other words, they have a certainty about what outstanding schools, and therefore their own school, should be doing.

So, what might these 'action-based imperatives' be?

THE CURRICULUM

Section One of the Education Reform Act (1988) requires schools to provide, and states that all students are entitled to, a broad and balanced curriculum, which: 'Promotes the spiritual, moral, cultural, mental and physical development of pupils and of society and prepares such pupils for the opportunities, responsibilities and experiences of adult life.'

Broad and balanced should be encapsulated and addressed by the curriculum being based on the eight defined areas of experience:

- expressive, aesthetic and creative;
- linguistic and literary;
- mathematical;

- physical;
- scientific;
- social, environmental, political and economic;
- spiritual and moral;
- technological.

Underpinning 'broad and balanced' is, of course, equal access, and head teachers must also guarantee equality of access to the curriculum for all students regardless of gender, ethnicity, disability, social and economic status, age and level of attainment.

So what of students with special educational needs? These SEN students are defined by the 1993 Act as:

- having significantly greater difficulty in learning than the majority of children of the same age; or
- having a disability which precludes his or her use of the educational facilities.

Despite this special need, they should have the same curriculum entitlement as all other students, and the need for differentiation (making sure that the delivery of the lesson is at the correct level and pace for *all* the students in the classroom) is paramount.

The curriculum should also:

- be 'relevant' in that it is accepted by students and parents, as well as teachers, as meeting their immediate and long-term needs in as interesting a way as possible;
- be 'coherent' in that it 'makes sense of the parts', supports the core purpose of the school, facilitates progression and continuity, and enables individual elements to support and reinforce each other;
- avoid 'unnecessary repetition' and build on prior learning;
- base 'progression and continuity' on an assessment of what the student knows, understands and can do;
- be challenging and stretch students to fully realise their potential.

Many teachers came into the profession to 'make a difference' to the lives of young people, and through them to the community and to society in general, and while there are times when we in schools get blamed for everything – from a lack of basic skills to teenage pregnancies – we should have a vision, which reflects a value system, which is at the heart of all that we try to do.

So the 1988 Act is not just the unrealistic pontificating of politicians. This concept of an 'entitlement curriculum' should actually mean something in practice so that all students can:

- develop lively, enquiring minds and the ability to question and argue rationally;
- acquire understanding, knowledge and skill relevant to their present needs and to future patterns of employment, family life and community involvement;
- use language, number and technology effectively;
- develop motivation and commitment, the capacity to learn from success and from failure, and the readiness to persevere;
- become reflective, aware of their inner self, and develop their own beliefs;
- develop a sensitivity to the aesthetic experience;
- develop an understanding of, and commitment to, commonly held values such as justice and intellectual freedom;
- develop their own moral framework;
- critically and sympathetically consider the beliefs and values of others;
- become socially competent, and able to think and express themselves creatively;
- appreciate and celebrate human achievements and aspirations;
- develop a critical awareness of the world in which they live and to recognise the interdependence and co-responsibility of individuals, groups and nations, for each other and for the natural environment;
- develop a zest for life and the courage and desire to use and extend what they learn.

This long list will only become a reality in those schools that recognise the need to focus on the individual, while at the same time celebrating and embracing the inherent 'different-ness' that exists among students and staff.

Systemic (driven by systems and structures) solutions are, of course, part of the make-up of good schools, but the importance of differentiated and targeted teaching in the pursuit of independent and effective learning is crucial, and good senior leaders are very aware of this. For example, differentiation within a set/ability grouping of students is even more important than within a mixed-ability group.

All staff in school should know not to assume that all students have an equal:

- starting point – early low attainment in literacy can dramatically affect access to the curriculum throughout a student's school life, as can a date of birth late in the academic year;
- access to facilities, encouragement or educational resources for homework and for revision;
- measure of security in their emotional lives;
- knowledge of how they learn – they have to be taught this skill.

Good schools will have active pastoral systems that make clear at all times, and to all students, that they are much more than a number on a register.

In these schools there is no perceptible pastoral/academic divide. The whole staff will also recognise that 'pastoral' and 'academic' are two sides of the same coin and that everything that the school does must be linked to learning.

A balance has to be struck between our desire as adults who have chosen to work with young people to ensure that those young people are happy and safe, and the inescapable fact that we have a primary duty to ensure that no student leaves our care having underachieved academically.

So, to summarise:

- the students are all different from one another and this should be recognised and catered for;
- everything we do in our best schools emphasises to all students that we care deeply about them as people, but that our primary duty to them is as learners.

The above are essential if we are to do the very best for the students that we teach. However, we will always be settling for much less than second best if we do not realise and have strategies for the fact that the students themselves are the largely untapped resource that provides the very best solution.

Teachers will agree that the student who thinks about their own strengths and weaknesses, and who is not simply a follower and a conduit for the thoughts and actions that originate from and 'belong' to their teacher, is a powerful force for learning. This student fully appreciates and can articulate what they can do, what they understand and know, *and* what they need to do to bring about sufficient progress in knowledge, understanding and skill, within a pre-agreed period of time.

Give them the skills and knowledge to drive their own learning. Spend more time with them learning how to learn, and the student will reach heights of achievement and self-esteem that were previously thought impossible.

So:

- All departments and faculties and year groups in primary schools will need to produce, and make available to students and parents, descriptors of their level/grade in non-jargon, student friendly and accessible language – teachers must be content to sacrifice a degree of accuracy, for the sake of clarity and understanding for the student and parent.
- Attempts must be made to modify reports so that they display and highlight these descriptors – this should happen automatically once the teacher types in the level and sublevel for their subject.
- Perhaps most importantly, we need to articulate precisely the difference between current attainment level and target attainment level.

The student needs the best information possible about what they can do, understand and know *now*. In this way they can be helped to understand what they need to do, so that they can do, understand and know enough to reach the target level. The *difference* between sublevels and levels becomes the focus.

The student should have a place at the decision-making table and this needs to become much more of a reality in our schools despite the undoubted fact that it is a concept that has its problems, and some teachers may well see it as relinquishing control and discipline.

However, those adults that feel that the vast majority of the students will at least welcome their elevation to co-conspirator in their own learning may be disappointed.

Young people in secondary schools and older young people in primary schools hate to be different from their peers; they have to 'fit in' in the way they dress, talk and behave. We all remember, usually with a wince, this adolescent chapter in our lives. We should thus not be shocked when they won't all willingly leave the pack to become relatively individual in their learning needs and requirements.

Some schools, I regret to say, have, usually subconsciously, adopted this 'don't single anybody out' ethos. In secondary schools the justification/excuse for this is that the student seen to be different to their peers will be seen as teacher's pet and bullied; in primary it is often a misguided view that competition is a bad thing. Whatever the reasons may be, the reality of school custom and practice will not have escaped the children in the school and it will become a part of the 'hidden curriculum' of that school; a hidden curriculum that is far from insignificant.

Equality for adults shouldn't be about uniformity and all striving to be 'the same', and I venture to suggest that there is great pressure on schools to *guarantee* equality when it comes to certain groupings such as race and gender. The drive for equal opportunities in general, but perhaps particularly in terms of gender and race, has done far more good than it has done harm, but its application has occasionally worked against its objectives in schools, and the more recent focus on gender bears some responsibility, in my view, for boys' underachievement.

The very fact that anybody, particularly a man, has to be quite brave to consciously open up this particular can of worms is, in itself, significant. Boys are collectively different from girls, and while a school must do nothing that harms the chances of success for girls, there is nothing wrong with unashamedly targeting boys using strategies that are boy-orientated.

Schools should make clear that it is all right to be male and boys have every right to be proud of their 'boy-ness'. Correctness, not political correctness, should be uppermost in our minds. So here goes.

Girls are, generally speaking, more mature than boys and they like to do things well. Boys are more immediate and predisposed to doing lots of things quickly, with more regard to quantity and being the first one to finish. Girls have a greater propensity to deal with the inevitable set backs, and boys work very hard to develop avoidance strategies. The 'audience' is particularly important to boys and a boy needs to feel that the people 'watching' see learning as 'cool'. Mothers are usually much more involved in their child's learning and the lack of day-to-day involvement of dad (particularly in secondary schooling) sends a clear message to their sons that education is not top of the male priority list. Boys and men are competitive and schools like to pretend that they – the schools – are not. Boys are not interested in being 'organised' – they won't attempt it, and they are not good at it when they do.

There is also a gender bias with literacy that is a major issue in schools. When this is further investigated, it is much more of an issue with boys than girls and it is a leading cause of boys' underachievement. Detailed examination of literacy issues often indicates that *boys' writing* is at the centre of their literacy unease and is key.

I don't claim that reading, and particularly boys' reading, is not an issue, but I do single out boys' writing as an area whose importance, not least to self-esteem, is given less prominence than I would like. I also feel that we are poor at dealing with literacy concerns at secondary school and in the latter years in primary school because it is by then far too late.

Primary schools should have systems in place to:

- identify from birth the students in their catchment who are likely to come to them – LEAs should have, or know how to get, this information;

- contact the parents of the newborn with a letter of congratulations, a booklet describing their school and a friendly but firm outline of what learning they would like the parents to engage in with the child between birth and four;
- repeat this contact at the beginning of each subsequent academic year with age-specific materials, e.g. recommended reading, writing/copying sheets, numeracy sheets, advice on websites, etc. included;
- extend an open/on-going invitation to these parents of children soon to be on their roll to visit school and pick up new materials/advice;
- send the pack that is sent to prospective students also to students already at the school but in need of remedial work.

At the heart of all this is a sense of urgency and, yes, impatience. There is also a rejection of the need to keep the children all together academically so that they can be 'taught' as a unit.

'Fast tracking' has many detractors among secondary practitioners. It is almost abhorrent at primary and primary school leaders need to be ready to group vertically; to have children taught in ability not age groups; and to be innovative as to how this can be done. Small numbers make this difficult, not impossible.

So, if I am right and the learning of many 4- to 11-year-olds is not as personalised, and they are not as stretched as they could be, then the consequence of this is felt much more by boys who are already and naturally disadvantaged by the way schools do things.

My good friend Wyll Willis (Head of Wallingford School in Oxfordshire) has crystallised the following action points for secondary schools to consider pursuing to reduce boys' underachievement:

- A cohort (group) of underachieving boys and a cohort of underachieving girls should be identified.
- The cohorts should be sub-divided into smaller groups (no more than six students) and a mentor should be assigned to each smaller group. This mentor should be a man for the boys and a woman for the girls. The male mentor in particular,

should lead his group in some sort of competition – usually involving gaining points for effort and where 'bonding' is encouraged. These boys' groups should be given collective/corporate names. Often, the girls' groups simply need time together, and together with their mentor to talk and share concerns and strategies.

- The individual boys and group that are most successful in the competition should be given a suitable 'active' reward such as: go-carting, quad biking, bowling, etc.
- Periodically, all boy all male teacher, and all girl all female teacher, assemblies should be held. These assemblies should have a focus on gender-specific achievement – the 'other' gender (teacher and student) is discouraged from attending.
- Healthy competition between boys collectively should be encouraged.
- Residentials that, again, are gender specific, like the assemblies, should take place with all mentors attending.
- Training (on the residentials and on other occasions) should be delivered to, and devised by, gender-specific groups. This training should focus on: how humans learn, and how boys learn relative to how girls learn – again, the 'other' gender is asked not to attend.
- Bullying involving girls embarrassing and thus humiliating boys should be dealt with as vociferously as the often more physical boy misbehaviour.
- Maleness and femaleness should be openly recognised and celebrated.
- The fact that generally boys are different to girls in the way they think should be articulated and acknowledged in the school. It should also be overtly understood that while girls tend to fit more neatly into what schools expect and require, to try, consciously or otherwise, to make boys become pseudo-girls is not acceptable.
- Revision timetables should be prepared for all students in the cohort for the Year 10 end of year, and Year 11 mock examinations. The mentor should complete the revision timetable for each boy in his group and post it to him. Boys are much more disorganised than disobedient, and focusing on organisation will be surprisingly effective.

CURRICULUM TIME IN SECONDARY SCHOOLS

The secondary curriculum is divided into Key Stages: KS3, KS4 and KS5; and the curriculum up to Year 9 (KS3) is compulsory and offers no student choice. It includes: English, mathematics, science, modern foreign languages, geography, history, religious studies, physical education, information communication technology (computers), design and technology, music, drama, art, personal social and health education (D&T – design and technology – would typically contain resistant material, food and graphics).

KS4 (Years 10 and 11) has a compulsory element known as the core. This consists of: English, mathematics, science, PE, PSHE and religious studies.

Usually, a single GCSE course requires 10 per cent curriculum time over the two years of KS4. Science often takes up 20 per cent curriculum time because it contains physics, chemistry and biology. English is English language *and* English literature. Religious studies and PE are the two subjects insisted upon by government – PE has to be a minimum of two hours per week.

There is then a group of subjects at KS4 that the student can 'opt' for. These are, not surprisingly, known as the options and there are often four, taking up 40 per cent curriculum time. Sometimes, schools will extend the 'core' and insist that a student studies, for example, a humanity subject (history or geography) or a modern foreign language, or the school will decide that a student only needs seven or eight GCSEs and policy decisions such as this would result in fewer 'option' choices for the student.

KS5 encompasses AS Levels in Year 12 and A2 Levels in Year 13. These subjects need approximately 20 per cent curriculum time each and the most able students will study four – most schools also enter students for Advanced Level general studies. Post-16 students have some non-allocated study time and they will have some time devoted to 'electives' designed to broaden and expand their daily academic diet.

Vocationally orientated courses will be offered to all years. Students undertake two to three weeks' work experience in Year 10 or Year 11 and careers guidance is a central element in PSHE.

Knowing that the amount of actual school time devoted to a subject has to be of crucial importance, many parents might assume that this issue is constantly being revisited and debated. These parents would, I think, be surprised if a survey were done of our schools, since it would be likely to show no change in curriculum time allocation in most of our schools over many years. If this is the consequence of regular discussion and deliberation then all well and good; if it is more about what has become 'traditional' and not offending certain key members of staff, than about current student requirements, then this is unacceptable.

School SLTs should constantly be revisiting and reconsidering how much time is to be devoted to a particular subject area and, much more contentiously, they should ensure that they satisfy the needs of English, mathematics and science before considering the other subjects.

Again, I would speculate that the majority of parents would find the strategy of putting English, mathematics and science before all other subjects far less contentious than most teachers would, and I wonder why.

Both groups would agree that schools are part of a service industry and therefore everyone involved in schools should care about and listen to the collective parent view. If all subjects are 'equally valued' English, mathematics and science would not remain 'the core subjects'. The fact that collectively the public 'values' the three main 'core' subjects highly, indeed, more highly than the other subjects being taught in our schools, is a detail that senior leaders should not in all conscience disregard.

It is, of course, laudable that teachers of subjects other than the core subjects will, and should, fight their corner for curriculum time. However, given that there is not enough time in a 25-hour teaching week to fully satisfy the needs of all, it would seem self-evident that the last person to quantify and decide upon, for example, the geography time allocation, is a geography teacher.

Senior leaders should canvass the opinion of the subject specialists, but they should have no doubt that they are the only people in the school with the skills and the appropriate hierarchical position, to take, and manage these decisions.

This being said, the debate and process should not become all about 'amounts' and allocations. Curriculum decisions should be rooted in the quality as well as the quantity of work to be covered.

Senior leaders must understand that what they are actually doing is quantifying, as far as possible, how much learning is likely to take place as a consequence of their time allocation decisions. Their in-depth knowledge of which teachers and/or departments are underperforming then becomes a major factor. Clearly, less curriculum time should be wasted condemning students to an inferior learning experience while the school is supporting teachers to improve.

This 'put the best teachers in front of the children' criterion and approach is perfectly acceptable and will not cause anxiety in schools that actually are child-centred.

CORE SKILLS

> **We want to send every student into the world *able* and *qualified* to play their full part in it.**

I would recommend that all schools have a 'statement of purpose' or a 'mission statement' and that they miss no opportunity, subliminal or otherwise, to advertise it. The above 19 words have served me and, I think, the schools I have worked in, well, and I would recommend them. All of the 19 words are important but **able** and **qualified** are the main ones and they perhaps need to be unpacked a little here and now.

Qualified can be taken to mean 'having the necessary skills' but equally it could refer to 'experience', 'attitude', 'knowledge', etc. Clearly this is true, but I suggest that, unless specific differentiation and clarification are called for, it should be taken as meaning paper qualification and examination passes.

Able then comes into its own and tends to corner the market in all the other important skills, understanding and knowledge so necessary in the business of playing a full and active and productive and fulfilling part in today's world.

A caterpillar's job is to become a butterfly and not just a better caterpillar, and our job in schools is to enable students to grow and develop that extra something that releases them as independent, useful, functional and valuable beings into the society they will inhabit.

A curriculum based on areas of study will, as we have found, inevitably and rapidly become a subject-based timetable (particularly in secondary schools) and a subject-based timetable will inevitably be interpreted by the students as inflexible, with the skills and knowledge not thought to be interchangeable.

These timetabled subjects would then squeeze the life out of all the other desirable areas of study; the areas of study that are often the very areas of study that are so important in the drive of the school to fulfil the 'able' part of their brief. To make them easier to recognise and therefore easier to teach, the desirable, non-subject-based areas of study can be enclosed within a list of skills known as the 'core skills'.

There was some debate in fact about the name and 'core skills' became 'key skills' and then 'corkey skills'; but whatever they are called the six (ignore them at your peril) skills are:

- literacy;
- numeracy;
- ICT;
- working with others;
- self-evaluation and thinking about how to improve;
- problem solving.

More recently, 'personalised learning and thinking skills' have come to the fore and these concentrate more on personal qualities than on 'subject-like' categories. These important qualities lead to six 'types' of student and these 'types' are:

1 *Independent enquirers.* This is all about the ability of students to process and evaluate information; planning what to do and how to go about it. These young people take informed and well-reasoned decisions, recognising that others have different beliefs and attitudes.

2 *Creative thinkers.* These students generate and explore ideas, making original connections. They try different ways to

tackle a problem, working with others to find imaginative solutions and meaningful outcomes.

3 *Reflective learners.* These young people evaluate their own strengths and weaknesses, setting themselves realistic goals with criteria for success. They monitor their own performance and progress, inviting feedback from others and making the necessary changes to further their own learning.

4 *Team workers.* This is about working confidently with others, adapting to different contexts and taking personal responsibility. These students listen to and take account of different views. They form collaborative relationships, resolving issues and working hard to reach agreed outcomes.

5 *Self-managers.* These students organise themselves and they show personal responsibility, initiative, creativity and enterprise with a commitment to learning and self-improvement. They actively embrace change, responding positively to new priorities, coping with challenges and looking for opportunities.

6 *Effective participators.* This is all about students actively engaging with issues that affect them and those around them. They play a full part in their school life by taking responsible action to bring improvements for others as well as themselves.

All of these are, of course, important and, in many ways, more important than geography, English, PE, etc.

The practical point is perhaps that the subjects are clear and defined. The demarcation lines, some would say barriers, are relatively easy to identify and for non-specialists to understand. The subjects are 'neat'. All of the above, on the other hand, be it 'core/key skills' or the 'personal qualities list' are more imprecise and the manoeuvre of providing discrete curriculum time is less easy, many senior leaders in secondary schools would say impossible, for these. We therefore begin to use terms such as 'cross-curricular' and 'mapping' and it all gets, well, messy.

- *Cross-curricular* – This involves a clear and delineated timetable with periods and subjects assigned to those periods; but with an agreement among the faculties and departments that they will ensure that the Core Skill or the Personal Quality will be 'taught' and catered for and covered. In the same way that the American tourist spends a day 'doing' London, teachers are expected to 'fit in' and 'do' literacy or effective participation, etc.

- *Mapping* – This is all about making sure that teachers are doing what they have contracted to do; it also entails checking for 'gaps' in provision and filling those gaps.

Regrettably, all this lends itself to 'being administrated' and secondary schools are continually forced down the 'policing it' rather than the 'doing it' route; much more time is often devoted to mapping than to learning. Even in the very best secondary schools, all of this is fitted around the line-managed, subject-based curriculum in whatever time is left and when the needs of the 'real' curriculum have been satisfied.

Primary schools are less 'linear' in their systems, fewer barriers exist and often subjects themselves are taught in more of a 'find out for yourself' sort of a way; this then makes the above less of a challenge. Many of the difficulties encountered by secondary schools in trying to teach so called cross-curricular themes and skills do not arise in the primary school setting.

Unfortunately, the relative looseness of approach in primary schools also may mean that *evidence* of learning in the cross-curricular themes and qualities is harder to come by, and evidence of progress even harder still.

THE TIMETABLE AND DATA ANALYSIS

Outstanding secondary schools regularly revisit the timetable to ensure that it still serves learning and current need; bad schools slavishly follow custom and practice whether it works or not.

This is only common sense you might think. However, many professionals will recognise 'timetable man/woman' who has perfected the: 'it can't be done' and, 'the timetable won't allow it' response. Too often whether students, and more precisely student learning, could be better served by unpicking and redoing the timetable never gets past first base.

The truth is that the timetable is simply a puzzle that anybody of reasonable intelligence can unravel. The real skill is that of formulating the teaching and learning imperatives. These are non-negotiable and will drive the timetable to ensure that it really does serve learning.

My blueprint is:

- the timetable should be 'blocked';
- setting by ability should be encouraged rather than discouraged – where necessary, it should be insisted upon;
- regular, on-going, built-in assessment procedures must exist, and the formative and diagnostic use of data must be fully understood by teachers, students and, where possible, parents.

BLOCKING

This is the word used when whole year groups, or more likely, half year groups, are timetabled at the same time for a particular subject.

Clearly, a timetable 'blocked' in this way would enable individual departments to group by ability, gender, or specific short-term teaching and learning need. The departments would also be able to decide how long to persist with those groupings and would be able to change them immediately should they perceive a need to do so.

Blocking not only makes the timetable easier to understand by those who use it, not just those who compile it, it empowers classroom teachers to ensure that current system fits current need, and it militates against a one size fits all mentality and mind-set.

ABILITY OR MIXED-ABILITY GROUPING

Many who favour mixed-ability groups argue that students should not be 'labelled'; this is a fair point to make. Students are, naturally and understandably, extremely sensitive about their position in the pecking order and the disadvantages and drawbacks of labelling should not be overlooked. However, to construct a system that artificially and superficially 'hides' the label is not the answer, tempting as this may be.

Outstanding schools relentlessly pursue learning and never doubt that this is their core purpose. Whether a student is worried about being labelled, or the teacher is worried about the student being labelled, is not the primary concern. The well-being, happiness and self-esteem of students are, of course, of crucial importance if the core purpose is to be fully achieved. However, these factors, important though they are, are not ends in themselves.

Schools, teachers, parents and students are often guilty of confusing effort, good will and good relationships with attainment and evidence of gained knowledge, skill and understanding. A student who is working at a pace that is realistic but stretching, who is regularly able to demonstrate learning, and who not only enjoys progression and continuity but is well aware of this fact, is much more likely to be a successful, happy and independent learner. The student who is being fed false encouragement is, nine times out of ten, all too conscious of this reality, and is thus in fear of the day when the test is truly norm referenced and when the extent of poor achievement is revealed to all.

Grouping by ability, setting, is a 'good thing' if it contributes to and enhances learning. The real question to be answered is: 'How can the drawbacks of grouping by ability be offset and minimised?'

ASSESSMENT AND DATA

To be in the wrong set is no better, often worse, than to be in a mixed group, so the validity of the grouping for each individual student must be constantly revisited and, where appropriate, revised.

The purpose of assessment is to monitor, evaluate and review learning and, thus, progress made. Regular, on-going assessment, with regular movement between groups should thus be 'the norm', timetable blocking facilitates this, and teachers must fully understand the need to collect and use accurate and current data.

Regrettably, the accurate use of data in schools has often played second fiddle to the earnest and never ending debate and discussion about the data itself. In particular, teachers have a tendency to micro-analyse the detail and the inevitable variables involved, rather than to use a broader brush approach which would yield far greater insight and thus much improved results.

The 'use' versus 'talk about' equation for data must become 90/10 in favour of 'use' and senior leaders wanting to collect *and make use of* data should be ready to side-step the well-meaning penchant of teachers to allege inaccuracy and subjectivity before it happens.

So:

> **How do senior leaders establish a simple to operate and understand system of data collection and use?**

Assuming that the collection and analysis of data is 'sexy' to some but, at best, no more than an acquired taste to the majority, it is essential that the pivotal points of our 'system' are known and, ideally, understood by all.

1 *Subjective data* – data that originates from the student through their teacher and the teacher's professional view is pivotal. Much of this will, by its very nature, be subjective. Senior leaders should not only be happy to trust teachers to assess progress accurately but, in my view, they need to state loudly and clearly that subjectivity is not, by definition, a dirty word. This data should be:

- On-going, quantitative and SMART – where possible, testing must be: quantitative, involving numbers, and SMART: Specific, Measurable, Achievable, Realistic, and Time-constrained.
- Time-constrained – out-of-date data must be jettisoned at the end of the agreed period of time. Critically, the time period should always be short – typically weeks not months.

- Predictive/target setting – assessment must be preceded by a prediction of likely outcome. This should always involve the teacher and should often involve the student: aim at nothing and you will surely hit it.

Without this prediction for the individual student and/or individual class, the teacher cannot accurately use adjectives such as: 'satisfactory', 'good', 'outstanding', 'disappointing', etc. These are words that relate to pre-agreed and understood success criteria. They are words that students respond to and take action to maintain or improve, but they are often words that mean different things to the different people involved. Teachers must, of course, make regular use of them, but they must also ensure at the outset that all concerned have a precise and accurate understanding of the terminology. To do this, these teachers must have a data-informed view of probable and possible student outcomes; a view that they must, where possible, share with the student.

2 *Formative data and summative assessment* – a full and precise understanding of the terms 'formative' and 'summative', is much more fundamental to effective assessment than the incessant debate about objectivity and 'clean data'.

- *Formative data* is data used to inform teaching and learning in an on-going and built-in way, while summative data is a snapshot of current attainment. The case for the successful use of formative data is overwhelming as is the fact that the use of this data should involve the student as an equal partner.
- *Summative assessment* is, by definition, periodic and it tends therefore to be undertaken at certain pre-determined 'hot spots' such as the end/beginning of a Key Stage. It should be used to accurately make those all-important outcome predictions.

The use of data in primary schools is often dogged by the small numbers involved and this often causes adults who do not have a facility for statistics to incorrectly use data to make wrong judgements: '84 per cent of last year's Year 6 achieved level 5 in English, this year it was only 62 per cent. What went wrong?' Possibly/probably nothing went wrong; there were only 28 children in the cohort and, as such, a percentage is statistically meaningless. What is worse is that LEA personnel then come into the primary school to 'advise' using this misleading data.

Percentages can sometimes be used in secondary schools but, more often than not, the statistical approach for primary and secondary should be the same in that they should both use baseline data to calculate 'value added' and from this they can then decide whether their work is good and to be continued and built upon or bad and to be improved as a matter of some urgency.

In secondary schools baseline data, data to measure from, is needed early in September in Year 7 (primaries need Early Years Data) so that the school can measure, and therefore subsequently improve, value added: the amount of learning which has happened, measured against that which was expected (prediction again) and was regarded as sufficient for a particular pupil, of a particular ability, in a particular subject, over a particular time span.

Cognitive Ability Tests (CATs), along with Key Stage 2 SATs (Standard Ability Tasks) and NFER (National Foundation for Education Research) information provide a base line and, in Year 9, secondary schools have the Key Stage 3 SATs. In Year 12 and Year 13 we have available ALIS (Advanced Level Information System) and/or ALPS (A Level Prediction Service) data, which predicts AS or A2 grade given the known actual performance at GCSE. AS Levels are studied in Year 12 and are half the content of A2 which follow on from AS and are studied in Year 13.

Increasingly, schools are using (pre-16) Fischer Family Trust (FFT) data. This puts together most of the above and makes likely outcome predictions for each individual student and subject.

FFT provides a choice to schools with four possible sets of outcome data for each specific school, and the school can choose on which of the four 'categories' it intends to focus, to define student progress:

- FFTA – 'to be the same as the progress made by all pupils nationally';
- FFTB – 'to be the same as the progress made by pupils in similar schools';
- FFTC – 'to be consistent with the overall improvement to achieve LEA targets';
- FFTD – 'to be similar to the progress made by the pupils in the "top 25 per cent" of schools nationally last year'.

Clearly, the 'category' the school, the teacher and the student choose to target is an indication of how 'aspirational' they intend to be and thus how high their expectations are.

In outstanding schools, informed predictions for long-term and short-term targets that shape teaching, and are devised and shared with students, are commonplace and accepted custom and practice.

Teachers in these schools also realise that these targets must be fluid and ever-changing if the process of target setting is to facilitate, and not bind, learning. Ambition is a prerequisite to real success and an 'I worked out my targets in September so I don't really have to think about them again until July', approach will suffocate freshness and vibrancy as much as having no targets at all.

The data must therefore be 'crunched' – made user friendly – and made available very rapidly; and it must be used repeatedly to revisit and redraft all targets.

INDEPENDENT GRADING SYSTEMS AND CONVERSION RATES

From September 2007 Ofsted began to judge schools on: 'How effectively leaders and managers use **challenging targets** to raise standards.'

I fear that this will still be rather more to do with 'how much' than 'how used' especially now that inspections have been curtailed to two days. Virtually all schools nowadays *do* have a great deal of data and teachers and senior leaders do spend a lot of time discussing that data. Despite the correct and laudable aim, Ofsted may just be reporting on a commitment to data use rather than a working reality.

Several of the schools that have interrogated the available data and the available expertise for making sense of that data (Fischer, etc.) have spent considerable time and effort asking themselves how to *use* the information gained to set **realistic** and **challenging** targets for *all* subjects and *all* children, and have come to the conclusion that they have to devise their own independent systems and that the 'one size fits all' approach is too broad brush.

What follows is my own take on this and I commend it to you; in secondary schools you will need:

For current Years 7–11:
- actual KS2 SATs sub-levels for English, maths and science;
- actual KS3 SATs sub-levels for English, maths and science (where possible).

For the previous Year 11 cohorts:
- actual GCSE results in all subjects for the past three years;
- the actual KS2 and KS3 levels for these Year 11 students for the past three years.

You can then produce a 'likely' and an 'aspirational' target in all subjects for all students by using the unique and specific assessment outcomes of cohorts of your students from previous years. The data is based on *your* school and not on national data. It *does not* preclude you comparing summative outcomes with the national picture; it *does* focus on the *use* of *your* data created *within* your school.

The process all hinges on **conversion rates**. If we focus on students entering your school with a Key Stage 2 level and sub-level of 4a (a, b, c, with a 'above' b and b 'above' c) in English, your data can tell you the percentages of Year 9 students *in your school* that converted, for example, an English 4a to 6a in the previous three years. You can then make subjective assumptions based on this data. If, for example, 57 per cent converted 4a to 6b and 20 per cent converted 4a to 6a, then you could decide with justification that the 'likely' target for *all* of your Year 7 pupils in three years' time will be 6b in English. Using the same reasoning, the 'aspirational' target will be 6a.

Clearly there is 'aspiration' in both the likely and aspirational target and there is subjectivity in the whole process. However, this is **formative** target setting and inherently in tune with the twin objectives of *use* of data and *use* of data to enhance student progress.

All other approaches are inherently **summative** and there is then a need and a requirement to think of clever ways to create a bridge from summative to formative use. Use of conversion rates has no need to contrive links; they are already there.

The same can be done at KS4 using KS3 levels and sub-levels as the baseline and GCSE actual results from previous years as the likely and aspirational outcome template.

Using conversion rates and known baselines and outcomes for all students in maths, English and science, secondary schools can produce aspirational and likely targets in Year 9 and Year 11 for these three subjects. To develop realistic targets in these subjects in the other years of each Key Stage, I recommend assuming uniform progress.

You should assume that, for example, five sub-levels progress over five terms is one sub-level per term. So, a student who has a likely target of 7b in May of Year 9 and is a 4a student in September of Year 7 will have a Year 7 target of 5a, and a Year 8 target of 6a. If in your school previous conversion rates say that a Year 7 4a is likely to convert to a 6a then the Year 7 target is 5b and the Year 8 target is 6c.

In order to cater for subjects that do not have an external examination set, you will need to satisfy yourself that the English, maths and science targets are, or are not, sufficiently close to the targets that would have been generated for these other subjects had there been an examination. With this in mind, I would suggest that the English targets are functional enough for: religious studies, geography and history. I would use the maths targets for ICT.

I would assign the English targets also to: art, music, drama, design and technology (food and resistant material), physical education and modern foreign languages. However, I would then ask the heads of departments and/or faculty leaders for these subjects working with and through their teachers to make recommendations to senior leaders to change those targets that they don't agree with to a suitable target for their subject. These subjects have, I think, a 'natural talent' aspect and this approach is from a senior leader's point of view.

At Key Stage 5 a formative alternative to the summative data assessment packages on the market would be to use a combination of an average points score derived from a student's *best six* subjects including English and maths together with a calculation of school performance over the previous three years at KS4 for the specific subject in question, together with a weighting for the specific grade achieved at GCSE in that subject. The data crunching packages that schools can buy tend to produce for each student an average points score across all subjects at GCSE and then use this to predict an actual specific target at AS and A2 for an actual specific subject. This does not take account of any unique aptitude for that subject that the student might have, and can be misleading as a result.

Senior leaders can also use their own independent grading system to either predict overarching percentages such as five A*–C grades or, indeed, to start with these and work back to decide what the targets should be to achieve these outcomes.

Similarly all reporting will be relative to the publicly stated grades. I would recommend telling parents the likely and aspirational targets at the beginning of each year and, from then on, comparing progress with the aspirational targets only. The report would give effort and attainment data and the attainment data would say: 'On target'; 'Below Target'; 'Working well towards a very aspirational target', etc.

If a student is continually well below or above target, then the target can be modified. However, I would strongly advise that this is an SLT decision and a decision taken in the full knowledge of how the target was arrived at in the first place and the reasons for underperformance, be they student or teacher related.

There is absolutely no reason why primary schools could not also adopt a similar approach. More of it would be dependent on teacher assessment and less on actual examination performance, and much would depend on an accurate assessment of the child's ability upon arrival in the school; but this 'conversion rate approach' is just as applicable to the primary context as to the secondary.

However, be it primary or secondary, this system enables a school to work towards an outcome that will raise standards and it provides staging posts along the way from which senior leaders, teachers, parents and children can make informed decisions. It is on-going, it is built-in, it is far less periodic, it gives the users the opportunity to adjust where and, more importantly, *when*, they need to.

THE RESIDUAL

This is the grade a student achieved in a particular subject, relative to the grade that student achieved in all subjects taken by him/her including the subject under scrutiny. Note that the residual is a measure of student against him or herself – a 'low-ability' student can, and often does, achieve a positive residual.

The formative use of summative data, and specifically the use of 'the residual', is in my opinion a much underestimated skill. It can be a very powerful mechanism for senior leaders and middle managers to employ, not only to raise achievement, but to get quick 'wins' and to change and improve the traditions and culture of their school.

Consider, for example, secondary school student X who gets one D grade ('worth' 4 points), four C grades (5 points each), two B grades (6 points each), and two A grades (7 points each). The student's total score is 50 points; average points = 5.55 (50/9). The D grade subject for student X, therefore, has a residual of –1.55. The B grade has a residual of +0.45, and so on.

This data can then be used to compare and contrast the performance of students and of teaching groups within a subject and the performance of teachers of that subject. It can also be used to compare subjects. Residuals based on internal testing can be measured against actual public examination residuals, and a view can then be taken as to the accuracy, and therefore usefulness, of these internal tests.

In this way senior leaders can form an objective view that will enable them to question faculty leaders, heads of departments, teachers and students with specificity, focus and precision. This comparison also enables senior leaders to require informed answers, and to decide upon a course of action to avoid and/or reduce individual student underachievement. It is not unreasonable for professionals to be required to explain why a specific student, in a specific class, taught by a specific teacher, is achieving less than that student is achieving in all other subjects studied.

This formative use of summative data thus enables, empowers and requires senior leaders in the school to exert pressure on colleagues to 'do better'.

RANKING

The key principle in data use is the opportunity to lucidly compare student with student, subject with subject, and teacher with teacher. Ranking is a natural extension of this and it is necessary if these 'comparisons' are to have the precision and lucidity required to raise student attainment for all.

Schools that are genuinely student centred and who relentlessly pursue learning as their core purpose are prepared to 'rank' subjects by residual and, once done, there is absolutely no reason why this information should not be available to all staff and governors. All heads of department and senior leaders should also be well aware of the ranking positions of their teachers.

Accountability that is fixed on fear rather than challenge will not work, but to shun accountability just because it is unpopular is unacceptable. The very best leaders are exceptionally well informed but they are, at the same time, supportively inquisitorial. The necessity to be adversarial and judgemental is very rare.

PACE AND TIMING

In secondary schools, a formal comparison of data should be done just after: Year 9 SATs for English, mathematics and science; Year 10 end of year tests; Year 11 mocks; and the GCSE examinations themselves.

To do this effectively, the data must be current and senior leaders will need to quickly collect and collate all data post-testing. They must 'grade' this data and then document the residuals for individual students, individual classes and individual subjects. The turn-around period for this must be days not weeks. Sharply focused meetings between faculty leaders, department heads and senior leaders can then be arranged to take place over no longer than a two-week period. The conclusions and action points that arise from these meetings should then be used and immediately put into effect.

STAFFING

Staffing is a major responsibility of senior and middle leaders. For head teachers, it is the most important task and duty.

Clearly, the objective is to appoint as many high-quality teachers and support staff as the budget will allow, so that class sizes can be reduced and teachers can concentrate on what they do best – teaching. Anybody who seriously proposes that class size is not a fundamental factor in effective teaching and learning – central government have been known to allow this view to leak through to the population at large from time to time – has probably never actually taught.

However, where staffing is concerned, quality is once again, and increasingly, more pivotal than quantity, and even though it is tempting, a 'bums on seats' approach is to be avoided. Once appointed, incompetent teachers become a far bigger threat to the education of students than the original vacancy ever was. To be fully staffed is thus not an end in itself, and if the secondary school senior leader finds that those mathematicians are not available, other, admittedly unpalatable, courses of action are preferable to appointing a known poor teacher.

Senior leaders could, for example: tailor the amount of mathematics taught to the number of teachers available while continuing to recruit; go into partnership with another local school that is better able to recruit; put one teacher plus one or two support staff with two classes; temporarily pay certain key performers more until posts are filled; reduce the number of classes by increasing class size, etc.

Often a perceived 'lack of staffing' concern is more of a staff deployment issue and, in secondary schools, teacher non-contact time should be very wisely and warily managed. Each so-called 'free period' costs approximately £1,000 per annum and throwing these around like confetti will soon lead to vacancies and, consequently, the need to fill those vacancies.

Senior leaders need to recruit 'em; retain 'em, but most of all they need to use 'em wherever and whenever possible to directly affect the learning of students.

So:

> ### What are the tricks of the trade when recruiting and retaining high-quality teachers?

1 The head teacher *must* be present in all teacher appointment interviews. No other obligation, crises, calls on the head teacher's time are more important than their responsibility to put together the best possible teaching team, and this must never be delegated, even to a trusted and effective deputy.

2 The interview programme should always include an opportunity for the interview panel to see the applicant teaching a full lesson.

3 Strategies for recruitment should be thought through as quickly and early as possible. Teachers can leave their present school to join a new school on 31 December, Easter vacation, or 31 August. However, most teachers prefer not to leave their classes in the middle of an academic year so their preference is for a September move. Therefore, seeking a replacement for January often means picking from a dramatically reduced field. Easter is also less than ideal, and it is generally sensible to create an in-house solution during the academic year, while advertising in January/February for a September appointment. Since teachers have to resign by 31 October for a Christmas move, 28 February for an Easter move, and 31 May for a September move, it is often impossible to seamlessly replace one for another anyway.

This employment entitlement for teachers to move mid-academic year, is the major cause of the reasonable and understandable complaint of parents, that their child has had more than one teacher in a given subject in one academic year.

4 The importance of a high-quality school website in terms of the recruitment of young staff should not be underestimated. Young teachers no longer routinely look to hard copy literature when searching for a job, and a school that has no website, or has a website which is patently out of date and old fashioned, will find it hard to get their undivided attention. Time and money spent creating and maintaining a website will be well spent.

5 Information sent to prospective candidates should be as professionally presented as possible, and should be e-mailed as well as a hard copy sent through the post. Applications 'on-line' should be encouraged. Sending a CD or DVD of the school in action is a very good idea.

6 When planning and taking staffing decisions, secondary senior leaders should be aware of the need to have sufficient staff capable of fulfilling a connector role. It is extremely important to concentrate on appointing specialists – people who are expert in their subject and who have an infectious enthusiasm for it. However, teachers capable of joining up all the separate pieces of the jigsaw are also needed.

7 The interview itself is clearly of crucial importance and it is worthy of much thought and planning. It is not an exact science and the world's best interviewer will 'get it wrong' from time to time. However, after the lesson observation, which should have given the interview panel a pecking order going into the interview, the interview is the best vehicle we have.

This 30–45-minute conversation is all about fitting a round peg in a round hole and not about being 'nice' to the interviewee. Senior leaders have a difficult enough time identifying Mr or Ms Right without letting all sorts of peripheral considerations get in the way.

It is good practice to take notes, to attempt to get a gender balance on the interview panel, to think all interview questions through thoroughly, to try to give all candidates equal time and opportunity, etc.

Interviews should be friendly and all reasonable attempts to put the candidate at their ease should be taken. However, interview protocol is less important than making the correct judgement and it is allowed, indeed it is good practice, to ask:

- reactive questions that are not in the script but that are designed to give a candidate a chance to expand or clarify what they have already said;
- 'awkward' questions such as: 'I see that you achieved two As and a B at 'A' level, but only a third at university, what went wrong?'

Decide not to give them an easy question that would enable them to settle down and relax. A first question such as 'What makes a good teacher?' is preferable to 'Tell us about yourself'.

It is in everybody's interests, especially the interviewee, to explore and probe as fully as possible in the short interview time available. Interview panels that have doubts and that do not give the interviewee a chance to dispel those doubts during the interview itself because 'they don't want to offend anybody', are often guilty of denying the interviewee an opportunity, and the school the best appointment.

USING SUPPORT STAFF TO ENHANCE STUDENT LEARNING

All schools have 'support staff' and in many schools the number of adults employed who are not teachers, and the number that are teachers are not vastly different.

In terms of salary, however, there is no contest and in a typical secondary school the support staff budget is around 20 per cent of the teaching staff budget; teachers account for approximately 60 per cent of the total annual expenditure in most schools.

Recently we have had 'workforce remodelling' in our schools and the spirit of this is that teachers are to concentrate on teaching and not to be routinely asked to do non-professional tasks such as: collecting money, examination invigilation, cover for absent colleagues (teachers should do no more than 38 cover lessons per annum, but these need not be spread over the whole of the academic year, so no more than one per week is incorrect and simplistic) etc.

Also, Teaching and Learning Responsibilities (TLRs) have replaced Management Points and senior leaders can no longer pay teachers for tasks or responsibilities with little or no link to learning: teachers who are not on the leadership spine cannot be paid, for example, to look after the mini-bus, to organise examinations, to do the timetable, to fulfil a child protection role, etc.

Clearly these jobs still need to be done and, if teachers are not going to do them, support staff must. Senior leaders therefore needed to appoint more, pay them more and give careful thought, often for the first time, to a management and career structure for support staff.

How these head teachers and their senior colleagues approach this continues to have much to do with how they view, consciously or otherwise, the support staff as a collective unit. Do they, for example, lean toward the extreme that can be illustrated by the lighting engineer at a West End theatre? This skilled operative has a very real and unique expertise and even though it is likely to have a star-studded cast, the play is totally dependent on sound and lighting. The director knows how significant this supporting colleague is to the success of the business and the school SLT that has this model in mind when they think of support staff is likely to value them highly.

On the other hand, the school senior leadership might favour the inanimate object such as a Zimmer frame model. The Zimmer frame is undoubtedly indispensable, but it can easily be replaced, it requires no training and no more is required of it other than its presence.

So, if you are a teacher, which representation most fits your attitude towards support staff as a whole? Do you, I'm sure unwittingly, patronise your non-teaching colleagues?

How often, for example, have you heard male head teachers refer to their female secretaries as 'treasures'? Have you done it yourself? Is it wrong anyway? How often do you fail to inform in advance the teaching assistants you are working with about the lesson you are about to share with them? Do you ever consider how they can function effectively in that lesson? If you have been guilty of doing just this have you ever thought about the messages you are sending to the TA and, more importantly, to the children?

'Support' should resonate in our schools with words such as: sustain, strengthen, corroborate, endorse, safeguard and vindicate. So let's be radical. What if we were to start from the premise that *both* teaching *and* support staff have the *primary* objective of student learning?

Once we begin to explore this way of thinking the following tends to naturally come to mind.

THE LINE MANAGEMENT STRUCTURE

The teaching and support structures for both teachers and support staff should mirror one another, with equivalent positions in both.

- *Teaching*: Teachers work to heads of department, heads of departments work to faculty leaders, faculty leaders work to senior leaders, senior leaders work to the head teacher.
- *Support*: Support staff work to support staff who have a particular expertise in a specific area (compares with heads of department); these staff work to support section leaders (compares with faculty leaders); support section leaders work to senior support staff (compares with senior leaders); and senior support staff work to and with the head teacher.

Once in place, the management structures of both support and teaching staff must have communications systems and structures. There should be support section leader meetings scheduled in the same way as faculty leader meetings. Senior leaders should be present in both and there should be a commonality of agenda and drive. The head teacher should meet with their senior support staff just as they meets with their deputies.

In-service training should also be a feature of the support staff structure just as it is for teaching staff.

KEY DESCRIPTORS TO DEFINE SENIORITY AND CRITERIA FOR MANAGEMENT PAY STRUCTURES

For a school to operate well, the management payment structure should be linked with the role and not the person; simply adding extra jobs to trusted individuals should be avoided; the pay structure should be objective, coherent and easily understood.

Teachers

Teaching and Learning Responsibilities have a 'criterion' followed by three factors (a, b and c) all of which must be satisfied for a teacher to receive a Teaching and Learning Responsibility 2 payment (TLR2), and one factor (d) that must be satisfied in addition to the criterion and first three factors in order to qualify for a TLR1. This fourth factor has in it a 'significant number' of full time equivalent (FTE) staff to be managed, which head teachers are asked to quantify.

Support staff

Certain 'descriptors' (equating to the factors above) should be employed as follows:

- Scale 1: works 'under direction'; performs 'routine tasks';
- Scale 2: works 'under direction but occasionally on own initiative';
- Scale 3: routinely involved with 'more complex tasks', 'occasionally asked to lead and engage in a management role';
- Scale 4: 'first point of contact to solve problems', 'responsible for other staff or students', 'required to work autonomously';

- Scale 5: 'leads a key area or section', 'performance manager for a small group of staff', 'involved in staff induction'.

Points to note:

- Section leaders should be paid at least Scale 5.
- Any member of support staff paid on Level 3, which equates to Scale 4, can be asked to take charge of a class of children.

Scale 1 is approximately £11,000 to approximately £14,000 per annum and Scale 5 has risen to between over £18,000 and approximately £21,000.

There is then a Scale 6 (up to £23,000) that would only be distinguished for the post holder from a Scale 5 by the uniqueness of the specific post and/or the importance of the 'key area or section' to the work of the school.

Beyond Scale 6 are the Senior Officer (SO – up to £28,000) and the Principal Officer (PO – up to £40,000) Scales and here the key word for senior leaders to consider and evaluate is 'strategic'. These are the true leaders of the support staff in a school and their vision will be invaluable.

A large secondary school will have among its support staff: caretakers; lab, workshop, computer and audio visual aid technicians; clerical staff; receptionists; finance, examinations and data teams; behaviour support, learning mentors; teaching assistants; reprographics staff; pastoral support staff; classroom supervisors (non-teaching staff to cover when teachers are absent); library staff; and a port of call for ill children (sometimes still called a school nurse or matron). This group of workers is then often led by a bursar and/or a senior admin officer or site manager.

A primary school will have far less facility to appoint support staff and this gives them an in-built disadvantage. However, this often leads to a make do and mend mind-set and the primary head who has correctly assessed what non-teaching support their school needs must not see support staff as an area where 'savings' can be made. Primary heads cannot afford coverage such as that described above; they can, however, usually afford far more support staff than they employ and they are often more likely than secondary heads to unwittingly think 'Zimmer frame' when they think of support staff. This will, I fear, continue as long as parents are willing to come into primary schools unpaid and prepared to do whatever is asked of them by the teacher.

COMMUNICATION

Most communications between school and home are still hard copy and, regrettably, these letters are often poorly presented and full of 'teacher talk'.

However, this is not such an issue as you might think, since over 50 per cent of these documents fail to reach home in any case, and the parent is often blissfully unaware of the 50 per cent that do!

How many 'important' documents designed to communicate vital pieces of information from school to home remain in little Brian's bag, alongside the half-eaten banana, or are found papering the route between home and school?

In my experience, the families with whom the school most wants and needs to have a dialogue, are much more likely to have a Brian very effectively damming the home–school communication river, and, perhaps most surprisingly, very few schools have any strategy to do anything about it.

The immediate answer is the good old Royal Mail. Yes, it does cost money, and it is irritating when an on-site 'postie' should be available. However, when it is unavoidable, schools should pay up because of the greater good.

The quality of the communication then becomes the major consideration, and twenty-first-century computer technology provides the solution. Communication with parents should increasingly be moving along the e-route and a parents' intranet should be set up on the school's website. In this way, parents can access their child's own year or tutor group, perhaps their child's own named site where everything pertinent to him or her – reports, letters home, etc. – is kept.

Schools also need to realise the damage they can do by a poorly organised parents' information evening. Power Point and microphones (in secondary schools) are essential and 'the speech' must be succinct, on message and it must not exceed 30 minutes. The temptation to tell everyone how hard the teachers are working, how obstructive the government is being, etc., should be resisted. Get the business done, be available for individual questions at the end, be pleasant, and go home.

Parent–teacher consultations (parents' evenings) are an entitlement, and while the temptation to deny a meeting to some parents who are just going to be told to continue with the present winning formula would enable schools to spend more time with others, it is probably too high a price to pay. These evenings are therefore likely to continue to feel, particularly in secondary schools, like a cattle market, I'm afraid, and they are destined to fail to achieve the objective for many parents, teachers or students. Factual and formative communication will need to happen at other times and by other methods.

Increasingly, the student is the main receiver of teaching- and learning-orientated communication and, increasingly, that communication is being delivered using quick, to the point and direct high-tech methods.

Quite rightly, schools are investing in more computers for the students and machines are involved in more and more lessons. In a good twenty-first-century secondary school:

- All teaching staff will have a laptop provided, and every other classroom will have a projector hanging from the ceiling.
- All areas of school will be radio linked so that teachers can talk to each other electronically and instantaneously.
- Several 'bookable' classrooms furnished with 30 computers will exist where teachers can conduct an ICT based lesson. Two or three computers spread thinly in every room in the school simply never get used.
- Each faculty will have at least a couple of recharging, radio signal trolleys holding laptops, so that the computers can come to the classroom, as well as the students going to the computers.
- There are several technicians ensuring that the hardware and software work.
- There is a rolling programme of replacement and repair.

- There is a commitment to every classroom having an inter-active whiteboard.

In this way the computer becomes a tool, like pencil and paper, which exists to facilitate what we do in schools, rather than simply another thing for students to learn about.

Timing and pace is all important and a high-tech vehicle that enables busy students, teachers and parents to say what they need to say, when they need to say it, will tremendously enhance all that we do.

The fact that student involvement in the whole learning process is increasing has to be a good thing, but it is perhaps inevitable that teachers will assume that their increasingly fundamental communication with the student results in im-proved and enhanced communication with home. Anyone that has been a parent of a teenager will know that this is very much not the case.

So:

> **How do the parents really get to know about progress or the lack of it?**

The one word answer is: **REPORTS**! – direct communication between school and home.

REPORTS

Parents and teachers have a tendency to get frustrated with the young, and too often we resort, sometimes subconsciously, to telling them how badly they are doing. We do this despite knowing that encouragement works, and that most students need to know that adults like them, and care about their interests and aspirations.

It is significant that those teachers that are seen by students to give freely of their own time and energy – extra lessons, extra-curricular clubs and trips – are not only extremely popu-lar, but they tend to be very successful in the classroom.

Teenagers can be forgiven perhaps for thinking that every-one they know conspires to prove what they themselves have always known – that they are rubbish at everything and doomed to failure. Is it any surprise therefore that they so easily lose confidence and direction? Ask the vast majority of students about what they are good at, and within seconds they will list their weaknesses.

They could do with some of what the bumble bee has. The bumble bee, I like to think, has a certain mind-set. This very successful creature is blissfully aware that it is ill-equipped to fly, so it flies despite the fact that all laws of physics and common sense would indicate otherwise. All students are 'equipped' to some, many to a great, extent but a skewed and unrealistic awareness of their own lack of capability often prevents them, unlike the bumble bee, from even having a go.

Clearly destroying the student's self-belief and self-confidence is not our objective, but we do have a responsibility to 'tell it like it is' if a student is to become a stakeholder in their own learning process, and thus empowered to make appropriate and sensible decisions for themself. There is a balance to be struck if our approach and actions are to enhance student learning. The phrase I would recommend to teachers and parents is 'supportive realism'. A clear and precise understanding of this concept is key both because we know that it is all too easy to be damning, but also because it is even easier to be unrealistically optimistic.

Attempts to 'be positive' can, before we adults realise it, be taken to ridiculous extremes. For example: our desire not to 'label' students in schools led for many years to an accepted wisdom that setting is a bad thing; because students should be able to express themselves, school uniform became, for many, anachronistic and repressive; because students are at the heart of, and should be fully involved in, their own learning process, we were told that teachers should abandon reporting on their progress to parents in favour of the students doing it and, as if by magic, Records of Achievement (ROAs) were fashioned and made de rigueur. This was then quickly followed by the growth of a kind of professional mafia, who 'did an emperor's new clothes number' on anybody that wanted to pursue an alternative.

ROAs are the classic example of the pursuit of philosophy and dogma with no thought to practicality, where process drives out all thought of outcome. When completing ROAs, teachers were instructed, note the word, to address their comments to the student, and they were only allowed, note the word, to record positive statements about the students that they taught. Students were required, whether they wanted to or not, to spend hours writing a meaningful comment with virtually no information to call upon. Since they had little that they wanted to, or could, say, students wrote what their teacher told them to write, or they satisfied the system by writing how much they 'enjoyed food technology lessons' and what 'a nice lady Mrs Bradford was'. The intent is worthy of full marks, the reality is that it did, and in some schools still does, more damage than the reports system it was designed to replace.

Of course children must be fully involved in their own learning process but ROAs:

- cut the parent out of the learning loop;
- take excessive amounts of classroom time;
- generate a weighty document that fails to tell the students and their parents what they, remember the student being at the heart of their own learning process was the big idea in the first place, need to do to improve their own learning.

Of course, reporting in the 1950s, 1960s and 1970s was, on the whole, poor, and the one-word comment, 'satisfactory', or the practice of simply telling students how badly they are doing is indefensible. However, constantly and incessantly force feeding them with praise is equally, and possibly more, injurious to learning. That said, even these old style reports let parents into the secret garden of the secondary school classroom more than ROAs. This is a particularly worrying statement when one remembers that the poor old parent already had, and still has, a daily battle for information.

The conversation between parent and child, particularly boys, often extends no further than:

'How did you do at school today?'
'All right.'
'What did you do?'
'Nothing.'

Body language and tone of response almost always makes, indeed is intended to make, further questioning impossible and the parent has that 'no win' choice: to interrogate and have a row, or to leave well alone.

It is, of course, a defence mechanism for the student – information is power so tell 'em nowt! For the parent this information black hole is at best another stress-ridden guilt trip – 'I'm not taking enough interest in my child's education. Why can't I be a better parent?' At worst it is the beginning of the end for education as a family issue and concern – 'The school is in charge of their education, so I'll leave it to the professionals.'

It should be no surprise that there is much less parental involvement in secondary schools compared to primary schools. Could it be that these same parents have suddenly lost interest? Is it that the size and system-orientated approach of secondary schools, an often quoted excuse, is off-putting? Or is it that adolescents have developed a talent for keeping parents very much at arm's length and in their place?

Replacing traditional reports with ROAs was a 'solution' to a perceived problem that continues to fail students and parents in too many schools. The key question that should have been addressed when dealing with the inadequacies of old style reports was and still is: 'How can communication between parents, students and teachers be more specific and focused, and therefore target what each can, and should, do to ensure that student learning is improved?'

Perhaps I can illustrate by using the concept of a coach (the teacher) and a high-hurdling athlete (the student). The bad coach watches the athlete and tells them to: work harder, practise more, and 'be a winner'. The good coach videos the athlete, and as they watch the recording together points out that the athlete needs to be more upright at the first hurdle, needs a snappier stride pattern between the third, fourth and fifth hurdle, and is tending to fade near the end of the race.

On the basis of their analyses, both coaches devise a training regime. Which one do you think will be more specific, targeted and focused? Which one will the athlete understand more? Which one will lead to most improvement? Neither coach has any need to point out that to lose the race is a bad thing. Should they do so, either explicitly or implicitly, it would be unlikely to improve performance, and since the athlete is likely to have an overdeveloped and exaggerated concept of the dire consequences of failure already, it would probably just add to their sense of hopelessness.

Reports are a good thing. They just need to be:

- regular and on-going;
- evidence-based, focused and targeted on learning;
- well presented;
- easily understood and interpreted;
- involving of the student.

I will discuss each of these points below.

Regular and on-going

Schools should have at least three reports: two progress reports and one 'full' report, and one parents' evening per year, per year group. The parents' evening should follow quickly after one of these reports, and the student should be present alongside their parent/s or guardian/s.

Evidence-based, focused and targeted on learning

To ensure that these reports are evidence based, the school should regularly collect data – on both effort and attainment – and the effective and on-going use of ICT is essential.

Well presented

The progress reports can be completely computer generated and the full reports should be completely word processed.

Schools must resist the temptation to produce banks of one size fits all statements from which teachers make a reasonably apt selection: this seems like a good idea, but it produces reports that are far too wordy and impersonal.

Schools need to be fully aware of how powerful reports can be, and therefore that their effective completion, like marking, is a vital part of what they do. The emphasis should be all about doing reports properly, and not at all about the time that they take. A member of the SLT, where possible the head teacher, should read and write a comment on all full reports.

But none of this matters if the reports don't find their way home in the first place – post them!

Easily understood and interpreted

Given that we are going to all this effort and expense, the information in the report needs to be readily understandable and usable.

Good reports focus on attainment and effort grading, and on forecasts and advice on future practice.

Attainment

This should be based upon National Curriculum Levels (number and subdividing letter, e.g. 4a, 4b, 4c – a is better than c) up to and including Year 9 and GCSE grades (A* to G) post Year 9. Obtaining a Level 5c or better in science, a Level 5b or better in English, and a Level 6 or better in mathematics in Year 9 ought to be good enough to achieve a C grade or better at GCSE two years later in Year 11.

These levels are linear and, with a simple summary/explanation, easily understood. The temptation to make up one's own scale or to use complicated descriptors should be resisted.

Effort

Effort grades should be simple *and mean what they say*. Unfortunately, even in schools that have fully embraced traditional reports, the spirit of ROAs is alive and well in effort grades. As a consequence these are complex and confusing, and too often incorrect and, therefore, extremely misleading.

Most parents would imagine that awarding grades for effort can't be that difficult. They would be wrong. There can't be a teacher in the country that hasn't waded through the mountains of paperwork, and sat through meeting after endless meeting about effort grades. All too often the outcome is a compromise that has far too little to do with the end user, be that the parent or student.

Many schools now have just four possible effort grades, for example: Excellent, Good, Unsatisfactory and Poor, to avoid the middle grade of three or of five grades being Satisfactory and therefore to avoid the tendency of class teachers to plump for the middle when unsure, or desperate not to 'de-motivate'.

However, this four-grade system leads in practice to the teacher going for Good when Unsatisfactory would be more accurate. The problem with this is that, regrettably, parents have an annoying tendency to read Good as, well, Good, and to react accordingly.

So:

> **What should senior leaders who believe in home–school partnership and who feel that home–school communication should be less misleading, do?**

- Abandon the notion that they can convert and/or train their staff to use effort grades accurately.
- Abandon the notion that they can come up with a system of pluses and minuses, half grades or clever descriptors.
- Give each student a position for effort and afford this position pride of place in each of the three reports.

This last point works as follows: Excellent = 4, Good = 3, Unsatisfactory = 2, Poor = 1. Each student gets a numerical score that will lead to a position in the year group, e.g. 34/297. They should also get a position to show improvement or deterioration of effort, e.g. –10, this time 44/297, last report 34/297. There would be an explanation sent each time, e.g. 'any student in the top 80 can feel pleased by how hard they are trying; 80 to 120 – students need to redouble their efforts so that they don't lose contact with the leading pack; 120 to 180 – beginning to cause some concern', etc.

This 'ranking' means that the teachers that award effort grades inaccurately have much less impact on the outcome, because their individual grades are unable to affect the effort position in any major way.

More importantly, the reality of the need for students to work hard relative to the norm is espoused and recognised, and pressure is put on all students to try hard, and for some to try harder. Current effort then has a clarity and focus both in the home and in the school.

> **Does it label the student? Yes.**
> **Is this a bad thing? No.**

The temptation for all adults, particularly those, the vast majority, who have chosen to work with children because they like children, is to equate a child being upset with a child being de-motivated. We adults should be surprised and worried if the child who is not fulfilling their side of the bargain and is not trying hard, didn't care when made aware of this fact. So an element of sadness comes with the territory. However, whether or not that child is more or less motivated is a completely separate issue and should be treated as such. A causal link between the two is not a given. That said, 'sad' and 'disappointed', must not evolve into 'stressed'.

So let's define stress – something that all those people that use the word incessantly seldom do.

> **Stress is pressure which is perceived by**
> **the student to be overwhelming and beyond their**
> **control and influence.**

Pressure is a good thing, stress is not, and a calm and business-like post-report dialogue between student and parent, and student and tutor must take place. A dialogue between teacher and student should have happened before the report was posted.

Attainment ranking
Ranking for attainment can be achieved in much the same way and is also to be encouraged. However, this listing of students in order of performance should not normally be made available to the students, or to their parents. It should be used instead to identify anomalies, e.g. ranked 25th in English but 200th in history. Setting can, and should also, be used in this way, e.g. set one for maths but set five for science. These anomalies once

identified can and should be investigated and a course of action decided upon.

Involving students in their own learning process

If we are to involve students – and parents – in the student's learning process, we need to give clear and precise advice as to what they should be doing and why. This can often be done by the student's tutor. An example of a tutor/pastoral report is shown in Case Study 1 (see below).

This achieves, in my view, what the student and the parent require. It begins by summarising Alex the person as seen by his tutor; it carries on by summarising Alex the student. What follows is a clear and succinct 'to do list' for Alex, not his parents

---

CASE STUDY 1

Alex is a mature young man who is always well mannered and hard working. He has represented the form in athletics and football as well as playing for the school football team and for District School Boys. His attendance and punctuality are excellent.

Classwork and homework are consistently completed to a high standard and demonstrate his efforts in all subjects. He is making excellent progress and if he continues to strive for such high standards then I am sure that he will achieve the success he deserves in the SATs and in his GCSEs beyond.

Targets to work towards are:

- To revise thoroughly for maths tests
- Complete homework questions in more detail in physics
- To carry out research in more detail in resistant materials in order to help develop chosen ideas more fully

He is a pleasure to have in the form; very well done Alex and best wishes for a successful future ahead.

or his teachers, and it rounds off, as all good reports should, with an encouraging comment.

But what of the student that is not 'on message'? Consider Case Study 2. Here, the same format achieves the same outcome. Clearly Kate is more likely to underachieve than Alex, but her tutor is well aware of the fact that being realistic and honest, and telling the student and parent clearly that which will be uncomfortable to hear, is not automatically de-motivating.

CASE STUDY 2

Kate's attendance at school has continued to decline. Last year I expressed concern about her punctuality; this has worsened as she is now regularly arriving late in the mornings. I feel that it is affecting her performance in her school work as several of her teachers comment on the fact that she is not equipped for the lesson. This will seriously weaken Kate's chances of performing well in SATs and GCSEs if it continues.

Kate's progress in her academic studies is also clearly hampered by her poor attitude at times, as she can be awkward and frequently distracts others from learning. Lack of homework is also a problem which Kate needs to realise will be detrimental to her future results.

I expressed my concerns in Kate's report in Year 8 and feel disappointed that her teachers are still commenting on lack of equipment and poor attitude in lessons. She clearly needs to make a determined effort to improve this situation straight away in order to achieve the position in the year group of which she is capable.

Targets:
- Complete all homework on time
- Pack necessary books and equipment for school the night before
- Arrive on time for school
- Concentrate on completing all tasks set in class, not talking to others

Kate, you can do better!

The subject report, written by the teacher, should also leave the student much more specifically informed about their future role and responsibility and, on one side of A4 paper, a subject report should contain:

- a tick list to indicate: attitude, organisation, concentration, classwork and homework;
- current effort, position, grade and predicted grade;
- a summary of reasons for the present rate of progress and learning and advice for how to improve;
- a bullet pointed list of SMART, particularly time-constrained, targets for the student to achieve.

PREVAILING CULTURE/ETHOS

Teachers, particularly school leaders and managers, must be ever vigilant in order to ensure that a culture of achievement exists in their school. This is particularly the province of the head teacher, and the messages he or she sends – either consciously or sub-consciously – are extremely important.

The head teacher, more than any other senior leader, should ensure the following:

1 Given a stated belief that everybody in the school is there to work, and to work as hard as possible, those pupils who do not do classwork or homework, or do it in a perfunctory manner, or do not hand it in on time if at all, must not get away with it, and, in particular, must not be seen to get away with it.
2 All student diaries and planners are read and used properly. These diaries and planners must be of the highest quality and they should be as customised to the school and year group as possible.

Often students can't find enough space in their planners to write any more than a brief outline – title, date and where to be handed in, etc. – and the school should provide a relatively cheap and easily carried rough book. An alternative is to have a policy of using the back of one's exercise book for note taking.

This kind of detailed advice will make a tremendous difference to a significant number of students, particularly boys. As I have already said: 'most students who do not engage in self-study or who do it badly are more disorganised than disobedient'.

3 *Negativity is immediately challenged* no matter where it originates.

Our classrooms must be fear-free zones. All students need to feel that it is safe to make a mistake, without sniggers or sighs or behind the hand comments, etc. from other members of the class. This bullying, for that is what it is, can have a dramatically harmful effect on the well-being of children, and on their academic progress.

Negativity among staff is also not appropriate, and while any member of staff is welcome to debate policy and practice in the proper way, in the proper forum, and at the proper time, at all other times collective responsibility should apply. *All* staff, be they teaching or support, are in some measure responsible for the management and the leadership of the school. They have no right to abdicate this responsibility. Should they persistently disagree with the way the school is run, the professional next move is to apply for jobs elsewhere.

4 There is a minimum of rules, but what rules do exist are articulated repeatedly and clearly and are obeyed to the letter.

5 Often the first indication of a student being 'off message' is their appearance. This is much more noticeable when the school has a strict uniform policy. School uniform is therefore a sound teaching and learning tool as well as being what the vast majority of parents want.

The uniform represents 'work clothes', and it should, as the name suggests, be 'uniform' – choice is not central to the concept of uniform and choice should therefore be kept to an absolute minimum.

A V-necked sweatshirt, school colours, bought in school; white shirt; school tie, school colours, bought in school; black tailored trousers or skirt; and black shoes, no trainers, assist tremendously when trying to engender a calm, business-like atmosphere, and its enforcement enables teachers to be pro-active in identifying an inappropriate attitude to school and to study.

All teachers must see uniform as an aid to learning and they should embrace the fact that it is their responsibility to police it.

6 Success is overtly and effectively celebrated at every opportunity. Traditional prize days and awards ceremonies and assemblies should be a feature of the school.

There is an increasingly widely held belief in many schools that students would not wish to be singled out as 'worthy of praise'. If this is the case, then this should be seen as clear and unequivocal evidence of the existence of a culture of underachievement, and senior leaders who abandon such events in a misguided attempt to prevent bullying are complicit in perpetuating the very thing that it is their job to eliminate. They have handed over control of the business to the competition.

7 All acquisitions are high specification. For example, if computers are to be bought, they should be the very best available. All furniture should be of the highest quality, floors should be carpeted where practicable, caretakers should have a commitment to keep the place constantly clean and tidy and the environment should shout 'high quality'.

Lack of funding will inevitably be presented as the excuse for the 'make do and mend' mind-set. Indeed, there are several head teachers who regard getting the last ounce of wear out of furniture and fabric as a badge of honour.

However, the head teacher who gives stirring speeches about high expectation from the stage in a school hall whose windows are bedecked with curtains that are older than he or she is, should be told to practise what they preach.

FUNDING

Despite all evidence to the contrary, there are still those who are determined to bang on about the lack of proper resourcing in this country in education. The reality is very different and, importantly, it is now the schools themselves that largely control their own spending.

Each pupil brings in an amount of money every April; the financial year runs April to March and cuts across the academic year, and this quantity of money is known as the AWPU (Age Weighted Pupil Unit).

The cost of a student's education is deemed to be dependent on that student's age and in the Sixth Form in secondary schools every student is weighted differently from pre-16 students, and also from each other because of their post-16 subject choices – some subject choices generate more money than others.

An 11–16 student brings into the school around £3,000 per annum and, when the individual calculations are completed, a Sixth Former can bring closer to £5,000.

Many who have to find the money in the first place might well disagree, but funding is a major factor in the raising of student achievement and twenty-first-century schools, like hospitals, need lots of cash if they are to provide the service and generate the outcomes that society rightly and increasingly demands. The funding has to come from the tax payer so the spending of it is a very real responsibility that adults working in schools should, and do, take seriously.

Senior leaders, LEAs and school governors must use every penny of income wisely and to good effect. Clearly, the operative word is 'wisely'.

Some senior leaders proudly boast their positive outturn figure – money left in the kitty at the end of the financial year – as an indication of (their) good leadership and management. They stand guard over the stash, all purse strings lead to them personally and these strings are tightly held. They can usually tell you about money that they saved by being 'on top of things'. Often they believe that education in general and schools in particular are habitually badly funded.

There are others who either don't understand or don't care about finance, and these individuals, perhaps in common with those who care too much about money, rarely give much thought to, or link the money being spent to, the amount of student learning generated.

A third category, and the 'category' I would recommend, is the senior leader who understands the following:

- The buck stops with the school, and although the LEA will give sympathy and advice, it is the school leader's and governors' responsibility to use the income wisely.
- The school accounts need to agree with the LEA's ledger, and to say that the LEA has 'got it wrong' is to cover up one's own inadequacy.
- They are managing expenditure not income.
- All financial discussion, debate and decision making must be current and not historical – very few costs are fixed and all are subject to review.
- Value for money is a component of school effectiveness – knowing the cost of something is *not* the same as establishing its educational value.
- Nearly all the school's income is generated by AWPUs, and *must* be spent on, and for the benefit of, those pupils currently at the school.

So it is the duty and responsibility of the senior leader to spend, not to save the money that the students bring into the school while those students are actually there and can benefit from it. Saving for a rainy day is intrinsically wrong, and given the pace of today's government initiative-driven decision making, is almost certain to be unneeded and unnecessary when the day to spend finally dawns.

Arguably the most telling and significant concept is that senior leaders and governors manage expenditure *not* income. With this in mind, I would suggest that there are just three cost headings to understand and work with: staffing costs; capitation; and other headed accounts.

STAFFING COSTS

The cost of teaching staff in particular is a very high percentage of any school's budget, and a very clear understanding of the imperatives that drive this can help to clarify and make sense of the rest of the running costs. Senior leaders of secondary schools should, for example, be fully aware that:

- promotion points will not impact greatly on the overall budget, and given that most are necessary for the school to function, agonising on whether one TLR point for the history department is 'affordable' is not a good use of time;
- teaching staff are the school's most important resource and appointing as many good teachers as possible should be an educational and not a financial decision.

Software exists to project expected staff costs forward three and five years, but these should be regarded only as indicative, and *viring*, borrowing money from one cost heading for immediate use in another, is not only good practice but inevitable.

CAPITATION

Many, probably most, schools calculate capitation, defined in secondary schools as the money given to faculties and departments for on-going annual expenditure, via a formula (the principle holds good for primary schools). The formula itself, if it exists, will have weightings in order to cater for those subjects that have to purchase consumables (science, art, etc.), and an initial block allocation for the smaller departments. The formula is usually based on pupil numbers taught by that subject and is an attempt to 'be objective'; the whole exercise is driven by the notion of parity and of fairness.

However, the schools that profess to have a formula usually can't find it. Surprisingly, faculty leaders, heads of department and governors rarely ask to see it. There seems to be a worry by some teachers that if you ask too many questions you might find yourself worse off as a result, and by others – governors and senior leaders – that 'if it ain't broke don't try to mend it'.

Annual discussion and debate about this sizeable and crucially important amount of money – which, unlike staff costs, is totally within the control of senior leaders and governors – and whether it is being used as wisely as it could be to satisfy current school and student need, happens in very few of our schools. I feel bound to ask: why not?

I do not advise that senior leaders go to each departmental and faculty account and change it overnight. However, a calculation to reveal the unit expenditure per child for each subject area is one that all senior leaders should do annually. This simply involves taking the amount given to a department on 1 April, dividing by the number of students taught by that department, multiplied by the number of lessons each student spent being taught by that department.

Figures such as, for example, £1.95 for science and 65p for history, will be generated and this will quantify the 'weightings' that have 'happened' over the years. In this example, science has a weighting of 3 compared to history. Clearly, the figure won't explain everything but it will provide an insight that was not there before.

Senior leaders can then make informed decisions such as: whether post-16 education should be given a weighting or not; whether English, mathematics and science should be given extra funding; whether the subjects with consumables really do need the amount of 'extra' money that the weighting generates; whether departments and faculties should pay for their own paper/photocopying, etc. or whether these should remain paid for centrally; whether they, the senior leaders, should keep back centrally more of the capitation budget for departments and faculties to bid for, etc.

OTHER HEADED ACCOUNTS

All other accounts should be 'spent' with the same sort of inter-rogatory zeal, and senior leaders must not feel guilty about taking from these accounts to feed other whole-school budget-ary accounts should the teaching and learning need arise.

Centrally derived (usually by government) formulae, over and above AWPUs, are inevitably used to decide allocations to LEAs, and then to schools; e.g. money for Gifted and Talented (G&T) students. However, the school's senior leaders and governors will know their own specific and particular needs, and they should not simply continue to apply the same formulae as government, who only know the generic needs of the country's schools.

School income tends to be, by definition, a one size fits all commodity, and school expenditure need not, and therefore must not, routinely follow suit. So, given that senior leaders, SLTs or governors have an informed, day-to-day understanding of school need and of the resources available to meet that need, they are entitled – indeed, it is their duty – to use the money to maximum effect. This will require them to regard the budget as an entity to drive student learning, and budget heads as merely a guide to spending. They will then indulge in regular viring between budget heads and every penny will be put to good use.

Clearly, it is virtually impossible for large secondary schools to use the money brought in by the students for the on-going educational needs of those students *and* to achieve a zero outturn figure each and every 31 March. For a school with a £6 million budget to get within £30,000 is, in my opinion, quite remarkable – plus or minus 1.5 per cent (£90,000 on £6 million) should be the prevailing government advice.

The three-year budget has been essential for a long time and the government is to be congratulated for grasping that particular nettle. However, to officially insist upon and encourage 'being in the black' is to encourage the hoarding of cash, and government should not be surprised if much of the money that they are making available to schools sits in bulging bank accounts while children begin and end their schooling in relatively under-resourced schools. If government really wants the money to raise standards and to improve student learning, the concept that 'error' in school budgets is confined only to overspending must end.

6

LEARNING

'Our job is to deliver live babies, not to give the mother a wonderful experience.'

Outcomes do matter and it is right that these should be the most important measures of whether a school is successful or not. Senior leaders, LEAs and governors should welcome school league tables and they should strive to ensure that their school is near to the top in terms of raw scores or value added. Examinations tend to be how we measure learning ('delivering babies'); so examinations are the key component of school success.

Therefore, the question that should exercise the minds of senior leaders is: 'How can we raise attainment?'. Regrettably, and for reasons I will explain, this all too often becomes: 'How can we change our free school meals category?' This, and other manipulations, happens because schools are not only measured against national averages but also against 'similar schools', and the measure often quoted is something called 'contextual value added'.

The main measure used to identify and categorise these 'similar schools' and the 'context' in which the school is to be judged, is the percentage of its families that claim free school meals – to have a high free school meals measure is to have a 'disadvantaged' catchment (the area around the school in which the students of that school live). Thus, while a school might have poor raw scores, any comparison against 'similar' schools (contextual value added) would be likely to be more flattering the more disadvantaged the students in the yardstick schools are.

This preoccupation with league table damage limitation is rooted in low expectation; it will inevitably permeate and weaken. Senior leaders must resist it with all the dynamism that they can muster.

In order to have outcomes to be proud of, teachers simply need to know – with a high degree of certainty – that sufficient student learning has taken place for each individual student given their age and ability. If all involved in, and with, the school have this information, the politics – and the league tables – can and will take care of themselves.

None of us would dispute that all students are capable of doing well, and that an outstanding school with outstanding teachers will stretch all students so that each and every one of them does as well as they possibly can. Outstanding schools, therefore, are schools that have gone a long way to eradicating underachievement. To do this, however, we have to have a clear understanding of our baseline position, or jumping off point, for every student in every subject, so that we appreciate precisely what the student knows, understands and can do. Teachers are then in a position to decide how much *more* their students should know, understand and be able to do, at the end of every lesson, or at the end of a pre-determined section of work. Learning objectives, appropriate for all children in each class, can then be set.

However, we teachers are too often guilty of confusing our hard work with that of the students, and more than occasionally entertaining ourselves by trying to entertain the students, 'giving the mother a wonderful experience', at the expense of student learning, and all too often of student enjoyment – far too many minutes of far too many lessons are taken up by the teacher talking and 'performing'.

If our learning objectives are informed and appropriate, and the lesson is thoroughly planned and student-centred, then the students will enjoy the lesson and they will learn. The red nose and whiz bang stuff is best left at the circus.

Mike Hughes in his book, *A Policy for Learning*, sums this up by saying that:

- learning and learning objectives are more about making sense of information than they are about receiving information;
- receiving information is more about teaching than it is about learning.

Given this starting point, assessing the teaching and learning balance, as suggested by Mike Hughes, may well provide teachers with the stimulus they need to change their focus from teaching to learning.

UNPACKING LEARNING

The key factors for learning are:

- high expectation of and for student achievement;
- secured behaviour;
- very detailed planning;
- pace;
- variety;
- positive relationships.

High expectation is easier to say than it is to achieve. Some progress can be made by one-to-one or group 'counselling/mentoring'. Fundamentally, this involves us, the adults, encouraging students in the hope of generating ambition. This is a very worthwhile practice and its effect should not be underestimated, but its effect on attainment can often be transitory, and at its worst it can become merely cosmetic.

For high expectation to be a persistent force for raising student achievement, the students themselves must actually, and passionately, believe in their own capability, and in the realistic possibility of their academic targets being reached and, occasionally, surpassed. Drive, determination and focus follow ambition, they do not precede it.

For high expectation to blossom and thrive, the right kind of atmosphere has to exist throughout the establishment. It should be a place where:

- people genuinely want other people to do well and support is always available;
- difference is not only tolerated but encouraged;
- people adopt a 'can do' rather than a 'wait and see' approach;
- seniority is not used to prevent innovation;
- there is a sense of cohesion and corporate purpose.

In this kind of atmosphere, constructive criticism is effective and SMART target setting is not intimidating. Schools should be places where it is OK to make a mistake and where mistakes are more opportunity than threat.

However, this vision cannot flourish in a theatre of indiscipline. Few would argue that the tabloid world, where students throw chairs, swear at teachers, bring weapons into school, etc., would generate fear, and survival, not learning, would become the core purpose. However, despite what our less than even-handed and professional media would have us believe, these extremes, like hurricanes in Hertfordshire, hardly ever happen.

Disruption and bullying are very much a day-to-day on-going reality in all of our schools; indeed, they are the single biggest cause of student underachievement. However, bullying and disruption in our schools are less extravagant and much more subtle and understated than many adults would think. It is often referred to as 'low level', and it is many times more prevalent than the more striking kind. Teachers must routinely take pre-emptive action against it, since it is far and away the most damaging.

How often, for example, do teachers pick up on, and effectively deal with, the student who has skilfully replaced the teacher's learning objective with one of their own, and who is occupying centre stage in this lesson just like they have done in every lesson that day? Pity the poor youngster who has the misfortune to share a classroom with this 'live wire'; who is being deprived of their educational entitlement; and who is going to be unlikely ever to have the confidence, given the environment they experience day to day, to 'have a go'.

Disruptive students, on the other hand, typically will have a confidence about them – a body language and an intonation in their voice – that dares others to contradict. This student is 'in charge' at certain points in a lesson, and will exert an influence on the atmosphere in that classroom that will detract enormously from the learning of others.

If, then, a key factor in any lesson is student misbehaviour and, more specifically, if the cause of that misbehaviour is centred on one student or a small group of individuals (often one student is the leader of a pack), then a teacher must deal ruthlessly and decisively with that individual or group. Generating positive learning relationships, with each and every member of the class, will mean sacrificing personal friendships from time to time, but teachers have a duty to take charge.

It would be wrong to suggest that teachers who persistently fail to deal with subtle disruption are more concerned about being liked, or are too timid to 'fight their corner'. They are, instead, enthusiastically, often excessively, focused on what they are teaching (the content). These teachers, therefore, need to develop a greater understanding about the effect and importance of how they are teaching (the style), and how this impacts upon learning; a detailed knowledge of how learning takes place is essential.

In his excellent book, *Accelerated Learning in the Classroom*, Alistair Smith describes the workings of the brain:

- The brain contains neurons (nerve cells) upon which all thinking is based.
- Neurons can send and receive messages to and from other neurons.
- Repeated stimulation causes the sender neuron and the receiver neuron to move closer together in an electrical jump called a synapse.
- The more frequent the stimulation the more permanent the connection.
- The more connections, the more learning can take place by using, or connecting to, these pathways.

- The best way to encourage permanent learning is to encourage the use of higher order thinking skills, such as:
  - interpretation and application not just accumulation of data and knowledge;
  - opinion and viewpoint rather than factual knowledge.
- The brain can be considered as being in three parts:
  - reptilian (survival, territorial, attention seeking, the need to be in charge, repetitive behaviours);
  - limbic (powerful emotions, filters useful and useless data, governs the idea of value and truth, long-term memory);
  - neo-cortex (the place where 'thinking' takes place).

Interestingly, the brain is principally equipped for survival, not thinking, and at times of stress the reptilian part of the brain will take over. Early humans, when faced with some predator that was a bit miffed because it had missed lunch, through no fault of its own, and whose size was only matched by its speed, and whose minute brain was not a determining factor, would have been ill-advised to hang around in order to decide whether to negotiate. In these very harsh circumstances, very basic needs must automatically rule, and the pre-eminence of the reptilian part of the brain is, I think, a given.

In these more civilised times, when contemplation and not physical strength is in the ascendancy, our evolution still has a disturbing tendency to get in the way of our pursuit of very different objectives. We no longer, I'm glad to say, have to regularly deal with immediate and life-threatening situations. However, we do get stressed, and when we are stressed we are incapable of thought, because our reptilian brain takes over and shuts down the other two parts. So when we say: 'I can't think!' we are probably telling the truth. This would also explain how trying hard to remember something gets us nowhere, until we think about something else, and suddenly the original puzzle becomes clear.

This does not mean that teachers should be wary of putting pressure on students. Students need to be stretched; thought pathways need to be created and repeatedly used and re-used. However, a business-like but calm atmosphere must prevail where the fear of failure must be kept at arm's length. A high-challenge but low-threat environment is the objective.

Given the right atmosphere and conditions, the thinking part of the brain (neo-cortex) should come into its own, and this is, of course, to be encouraged. This part of the brain is divided into four lobes, and separated into two halves: the left side of the brain and the right side of the brain.

People tend to be predominantly left brained (language, logic, mathematical, numbers, sequence, analysis); or right brained (patterns, spatial awareness, musical appreciation, images and pictures, imagination). This will lead to them having a preferred learning (and teaching) style.

Not surprisingly a great deal of work has been done categorising these 'learning styles'; and one can choose from several different but related alternatives. Some, for example, would summarise learning styles via VAK (Visual, Audio, and Kinaesthetic). On average, 29 per cent of us are visual learners (can 'see' or visualise what they are trying to learn), 34 per cent are auditory learners (can assimilate very effectively what is said to them), and 37 per cent are kinaesthetic learners (can access learning by experiencing it or 'feeling' what it means to have learned successfully).

A desire to focus on the individual student's preferred learning style might cause the teacher to want to 'unpack' learning more than an application of VAK would allow. That teacher might well look to Gardner's Multiple Intelligences. This theory suggests that there are around eight preferred intelligences: Linguistic, Mathematical and logical, Visual and spatial, Musical, Interpersonal, Intrapersonal, Kinaesthetic and Naturalistic.

All of these theories enjoy the advantage that the data is relatively easy to collect using student questionnaires. It can then be made available and the teacher, student and parent can understand better the preferred learning style of the student and this may suggest possible reasons for, and solutions to, a lack of progress.

Perhaps I can illustrate this using a report written by a chemistry teacher for a Year 10 student in his class, shown in Case Study 3.

CASE STUDY 3

48% C grade at GCSE

Liam has grown in confidence this year. He needed to catch up at one point and has achieved this successfully. Liam's course-work is good and should be completed soon. However, he does not learn well when the teacher adopts a didactic approach, preferring to learn by doing. His Intrapersonal and Linguistic Multiple Intelligence scores are relatively low, and he therefore finds it difficult to naturally and automatically engage when he has to sit and listen to myself or to class discussion. However, there is a certain paradox here in that his Interpersonal and Kinaesthetic scores are high yet he rarely interacts with me or the class – his Visual and Spatial score is also high. He often seems to work at a slower pace than that required and he prefers to follow rather than lead. There will be times when the teaching style for a particular lesson does not fit easily with Liam's preferred learning style. However, he will need to try harder to 'engage' mentally at these times. When the lesson is more interactive and kinaesthetic – and this is often – Liam must take the initiative more than he is at the moment; he will have to work hard to do this consistently from now on. Liam will also need to approach the whole exercise of revision with more ambition and thought for the mock examinations which are scheduled for this December.

Good progress but we will need to step things up next year Liam.

Teachers will naturally adopt a particular teaching style and, while they will vary it, it will tend to follow a pattern particular to them. This is perfectly acceptable and indeed it is how it should be. Nevertheless, the teacher who fully understands the preferred learning styles of each of his/her students will be much more likely to make required and timely interventions that enable increased learning to take place.

Students, particularly boys, will tend to adopt a particular approach to learning both because it has served them well in the past and because they prefer that method. However, this does not mean that that student, or any other, is not capable of utilising the other learning styles.

It seems that only when we start paid work, and we have accepted that no one else will do our thinking for us, when we are responsible and accountable if things don't get finished, or go wrong, do we match our way of thinking to the task. At school, we get into 'school mode' and stick to that method no matter what: 'Of course I can do graphs in maths, I'm in the top set; but this is science!'. We are confident – and have every reason to be confident – at school that if we mess up, someone (teacher or parent) will sort it out for us. It is therefore very important that a balance and variety of teaching style is available to all students, and that they get used to utilising the most appropriate intelligence/learning style for the task rather than the learning style they prefer.

Learning has therefore to be taken seriously by SLTs, and while all members of this team will be thoroughly immersed in, and concerned with, learning, I would recommend that a least one SLT member is defined as 'director of learning'. This person would be someone whose expressed primary purpose is '**all aspects of classroom performance and practice**', and who would:

- define for staff what is effective teaching and learning;
- audit teaching and learning styles across the school;
- identify good practice re teaching and learning in school;
- set up systems to ensure the sharing of good practice;
- provide targeted quality INSET (teacher training);
- train appropriate staff in how to observe lessons – i.e. how to check that learning is taking place – and manage feedback;
- work with heads of department to devise systems for monitoring the quality of learning in the department;
- ensure that effective lesson planning is taking place with appropriate learning objectives set and shared;
- monitor the setting of SMART targets and appropriate action plans for students;

- ensure that the student and staff planner is an effective and integral part of the learning and teaching process.

Involving students in their own learning process is an essential requirement for good and effective learning, but this cannot happen in a vacuum and the process is severely hampered by the fact that the students, on the whole, don't want to be involved. The 'average' secondary school student, particularly – once again – a boy, prefers to have education done to them as opposed to with them.

Teachers must be in no doubt that they will have to take any and all necessary counter-measures to block or restrict the student 'opt-out strategy', even when it adversely affects the personal relationship and friendship that they have built with that student. In order to do this, teachers and parents need irrefutable evidence, such as the effort position, which enables them to:

- articulate and quantify the extent to which the student has become a passive bystander in their own educative process;
- dictate and decide when and whether sufficient learning has taken place given the time-frame and the student's age and ability.

There is a clear need to obstruct all escape routes, but this is only the precursor for effective student-centred learning. Day-to-day, lesson-by-lesson, minute-by-minute happenings in the classroom remain the most important aspect that schools have to get right. All schools should strive to 'get this right' 100 per cent of the time, but this is unlikely ever to be achieved. However, what is certain is that schools will come nowhere near this figure unless its senior leaders manage 'the classroom experience' in a coherent and consistent manner, such that all lessons in the school have a common framework within which the individual teacher and student can thrive. The rogue teacher who 'wings it' and gets by through force of personality, is no longer effective enough for our twenty-first-century schools, and has to be brought into line.

The director of learning will need to know what a good lesson looks like and this must be articulated to the staff. Some school leaders are content to leave the structure of lessons to the teachers and, while I would hate to stifle individuality and innovation at the chalkface, I believe senior leaders have a duty and responsibility to be clear and unequivocal about what they expect to see in all classrooms in their school.

REFLECTING AND REVIEWING AND THE FOUR-PART LESSON

Senior leaders need to discuss and negotiate, and then to articulate what is going to be 'the typical lesson framework' for the school.

My preferred option is the four-part lesson, defined as follows:

1 The teacher outlines (visually and verbally) the learning objective(s) for that lesson – this is what they hope and intend that all students will 'make sense of' at the end of that lesson, that they did not know or understand, or could not do, at the start of the lesson (five minutes of a 50-minute lesson). Note: it is *not* what the students are going to *do*.
2 The teacher outlines (visually and verbally) the activity(ies) for that lesson – this is what they hope that all students will do during that lesson in order to achieve the learning objective(s) (five minutes of a 50-minute lesson). Typically the teacher will 'model' what is expected/to be done at some point during stages 1 and 2.
3 The activity is undertaken by the class – this can be led or facilitated by the teacher; it can be in friendship groups or teacher-determined groups; it can be essentially written and in silence, or verbal and therefore by definition, quite noisy – managed by the teacher (30 minutes of a 50-minute lesson), but the teacher should strive not to be talking too much to the class as a unit.
4 The teacher orchestrates student reflection upon what has been learned (five to ten minutes of a 50-minute lesson). This last section needn't be at the end of the lesson, but it must refer to the stated learning objective(s); it must happen each and every lesson.

Reflection, and making reflection time available, is a vital component if what Mike Hughes calls the 'ah!' factor is to take place. This is the moment – or moments – in all lessons where the student is suddenly stopped in their tracks and the penny drops; without it the lesson is ineffective, in that learning has not been advanced and developed.

> **REVIEW:** To provide specific advice related to learning and particular learning objectives; this can relate to a specific lesson, but is more likely linked to a block of work studied over a period of time. It can, and most of the time should, be periodic (every now and again) and bolted-on.

Reflection is often confused with reviewing, and a clear distinction should be made between these processes.

Reflective learning should:

- relate to the stated learning objectives in each lesson;
- be done under the direction of subject teachers and, where appropriate, the student's thoughts about what they have learned in that lesson should be noted in their planner, or the back of the exercise book;
- form the basis of a periodic (monthly/termly) review of learning completed by tutors/learning mentors;
- mean that most lessons can begin by the teacher asking students to look at their planner, or their exercise book, to remind themselves of what they, the student, said they had learned last lesson. This can produce a greater understanding of the learning objective for the current lesson.

Reviewing:

- would be orchestrated and driven by senior leaders;
- would be done in a general, over-arching manner by tutors with their form – not with individuals in the form;
- would be done specifically and with precision by learning mentors with individual students;

- requires training/guidance for the tutors;
- would not involve 'pastoral' issues – teachers, tutors and heads of year would continue to pick these up, and would meet students for a one-to-one talk as appropriate.
- must leave each student aware of, and clear about, what they now need to do to improve their own learning.

Clearly, therefore, reflection has to be done by subject teachers. Reviewing can be done by tutors or, in order to ensure consistency of quality and approach, by learning mentors. Most senior leaders have realised that a team of learning mentors (non-teaching support staff) who review with each and every student, up to three times per year, and who put together a report for the student and parent after each review, is invaluable.

Reflection is the only valid purpose for homework, and while few parents are 'against' homework, there is a growing realisation among teachers that setting effective homework might be an activity that is much more difficult than one would imagine.

Homework arose in an era when classroom learning was poor and self-tuition was a necessity. Perhaps we are coming through this and our drive should no longer be to make homework ever-present. Our focus should now be more to make it reflective, engaging and forward thinking. Homework should thus be more about the application of higher-order thinking skills, and it should, as a consequence, be set less often, and then primarily for higher-ability groups of students.

THE DIFFERENCE BETWEEN COUNSELLING AND REVIEWING

Counselling is also often confused with reviewing and it is important that teachers and tutors understand the difference, and ensure that counselling is kept to a minimum on the occasions when the purpose is reviewing.

COUNSEL: To provide general advice often focused on the student working harder and improving the student's attitude and behaviour.

Frequently our desire to make students happy and to deal with their personal problems leads us to forget our primary purpose, and our 'social work' duties become our raison d'être.

Good schools have come to realise that their teachers must be fully aware of the need to separate pastoral and academic work. When this does not happen, it can, and often does, work against learning.

Increasingly, many of our better school leaders have gone further than this, and they are taking overt and clear steps to remove the hidden (or not so hidden) message to staff and students that pastoral work is 'more important' than what happens in the classroom.

Heads of year in secondary schools are no longer routinely paid more than their head of department, and many schools are employing non-teaching inclusion officers to work with the day-to-day pastoral issues under the direction of teachers who, themselves, are in no doubt of the primacy of classroom learning for each and every student.

Pastoral systems in British schools are a strength that other nations envy, and I do not call for a move to the French system, for example, where teachers teach and all other student interactions are left to non-teaching staff within the school. However, there is still a need to redress the pastoral/teaching and learning balance in many of our schools.

ASSESSMENT FOR LEARNING (AFL)

Put simply this is on-going assessment that takes place in classrooms and that is designed to engage the student in the learning process. It often puts the student in the shoes of the teacher, and the student becomes the assessor as well as the assessed.

Typically students will have the grading criteria explained to them, and then will be asked to grade their own, and often another student's, work. These 'marks' awarded by the student are then discussed and the student's decisions are 'unpacked'.

Structured class discussion and student groupings are also used to enhance student involvement. All these techniques have in common the proposition that the student is at the heart of the learning process, and therefore needs to know about every aspect of it.

EXAMINATION TECHNIQUE

AFL is to enhance learning and to involve the student in the learning process. However, it also tends to invite the student into the mysterious world inhabited by the creature known as the 'examiner'.

A clear understanding of the learning by the teachers, the parents and the students and a clear policy and practice for learning in the school is only part of the progression towards success for students. *Passing* the examination *does* matter and it won't say 'knew her/his stuff but failed to do enough in the examination to evidence that knowledge' on the examination certificate. We all know that England were the better team against Poland when Hunter missed that tackle in the second half that led to the Polish goal; but the score was one–nil to Poland and *they* went to the World Cup Finals.

Teachers do not have the luxury to equivocate about the importance of examinations and they certainly do not have the right to keep examination technique to themselves as some sort of secret handshake that only they can know. It is their job to ensure that students have the knowledge and understanding and skills *and* the technique to actually pass the examination.

Examination technique and active and, sometimes, competitive revision is not something that students can master automatically and under their own steam. Some will develop the necessary approach and skills and some never will. Those that do may well do so by repeatedly failing examinations and tests until the penny drops, those that do not will: incorrectly diagnose what they are doing wrong and apply the wrong medicine oblivious to its damaging side effects – 'I don't ever begin my revision until the night before because I find if I start too early it confuses me'; or they will simply give up and drown in a sea of low self-esteem and self-loathing. This last category of student is the one that typically has behavioural issues and its members are often described as EBD – Educational Behavioural

Difficulty students. Examinations are not going to go away; but if we spend time showing students how to cope with them, EBD just might.

What follows are just a couple of the many practical examples of what I mean:

1 If students have to learn lists, e.g. components of fitness in PE, they could be given a number/word rhyming list:

1 Bun

2 Shoe

3 Tree

4 Door

5 Hive

6 Sticks

7 Heaven

8 Gate

9 Line

10 Hen

The student then imagines a teacher (if it's a boy, who we're told thinks about sex every few minutes, perhaps a naked lady – if it works don't knock it!) juggling some buns. The word he is trying to remember is coordination. Shoe becomes a running shoe with spikes; the word is speed, etc.

2 Techniques for actually doing an examination paper would perhaps revolve around FUMFER and the teacher could spend lesson time on this:

F *Flick and pick*: flick through the examination paper before you start and pick what you are going to do first, check the instructions, e.g. choose and only do *one* question out of the four in Section 2.

U *Underline* the command word and match it to its meaning:

• Describe – say *what* is shown or *what* happens.

• Explain – say *why* something happens, give reasons.

- Compare – look at *similarities* and *differences*; use connectives, e.g. 'whereas'.
- Evaluate – *weigh up* the importance of something.

M *Marks*: the number of marks for a question tells you the number of points to make or the number of things to say.

F *Figures*: what type of figures does the question expect you to use, e.g. percentages?

E *Examples*: command words are often difficult to comply with: this becomes easier when you use examples to illustrate.

R *Re-mark*: reading through the paper when you've finished (advice that is often given) is difficult, and seldom complied with by the student. However 'marking' it is very useful and relatively easy to do in the 10 minutes or so after you have finished the examination and before you are allowed to leave the examination room.

Knowing, understanding and being able to do things makes us feel good about ourselves and makes us happy. Our quality of life is enhanced and our interactions with others are improved. Having the kind of proof that those around us recognise that we know, understand and can do things is particularly important when we are young because we have little else that is overtly and clearly ours. We are somebody else's daughter or son or brother or sister. To be the person that did well – in the best schools this means 'did one's best' and what 'one's best' means is precisely understood by all students – on their own in that examination room means an awful lot. The grade achieved does open or close doors of opportunity, but the depth and longevity of the effect of pass or fail on a young person's perception of self should not be underestimated.

7

MAKING THINGS BETTER: MONITORING, EVALUATING AND REVIEWING

MER: THE TERMS

MONITOR: To check, control, warn or keep a record of something.

EVALUATE: To find or judge the value.

REVIEW: To examine, look back on, to reconsider.

I like to think that things in schools improve because we the workers, as Jean Luc Picard would say 'make it so'. Perhaps they recover all on their own; perhaps, and we should be big enough to entertain this possibility, they pull through *despite* our efforts.

Schools and educators have long been the subject of criticism, and education is, more than ever, a political football and while much that is said, often by those that should know better, does not bear scrutiny, mud will stick. However, anyone that is really interested in finding out the facts rather than looking for someone to blame, will know that the objective data proves beyond all doubt that the day-to-day business in our schools has improved greatly over the last decade. Let nobody be in any doubt that we, the professionals working in those schools, are the single most important factor making the difference; and that that 'difference' represents real progress.

However, the caring professions can never be satisfied and we in schools, the Health Service, the Police Force, Social Services, etc. must always strive, perhaps more than other professions, to be and to do even better. To accomplish this we need to know with precision how well we are doing at present and how well we could do in the future: we need to quantify our baseline and our targets. We need to **monitor, evaluate** and **review**.

Monitoring, evaluating and reviewing (MER) are activities fundamental to the fortunes of all schools but they are very much processes to be undertaken rather than outcomes to be achieved, and unless they come as a package, one with the other, they will bring a feel-good factor for the adults involved – a feeling of earning one's money – but very little else. Three separate, different and important skills they might be, but it is as a team like Athos, Porthos and Aramis or, as I prefer to think, Charlton, Law and Best, that they score and score highly.

However, important though they are, each of these processes, or even the combination, does not have a divine right to raise student achievement, and the doing of them is, in itself, not enough. There must always be a clear and present and, where possible, quantified link with learning and therefore with student progress; this link must always be uppermost in the teacher or school leader's thoughts. He or she must be fully alert to the fact that an activity that has zero or even limited effect on learning must be regarded as time wasted and must, given that time in school with students is so curtailed and often incomplete, be eschewed.

It follows, therefore, that no school can afford not to participate in monitoring, evaluating and reviewing, but that all involved must fully understand these skilled activities; they must also realise that one follows the other like night follows day, and that their contribution to student learning and progress must be sufficient to make the commitment of time and effort worthwhile.

So, how can we better understand monitoring, evaluating and reviewing and how can we maximise their effect on student progress?

Since there are differing 'levels' of curriculum leaders working in and with schools: senior, middle, classroom, govern-or, LEA, etc., there are differing 'levels' of MER. However, the fundamental processes are the same and can be summarised as follows.

THE PROCESS

This should be constantly evolving, dynamic, on-going and sys-tematic, with conclusions drawn and action points and measur-able outcomes identified. The time-frame for progress should be clear to all involved and it should be realistic but stretching.

One MER process will follow but, more importantly, will be informed by, its predecessor and will thus become more and more specific and focused on precisely identified areas of strength and weakness.

Clearly, the ultimate aim should be that the learner should be immersed in the whole process of monitoring, evaluating and reviewing and the trio should become *self*-monitoring, *self*-evaluating and *self*-reviewing. However, school leaders should be wary of pursuing this too soon. Monitoring, evaluating and reviewing are intrinsically activities that are done *to* rather than done *with* and the need (particularly at the beginning), indeed the requirement, for a 'top-down' approach should be clearly understood.

So, in order to better appreciate MER, if we focus on second-ary senior leaders and their need to devise and implement a Curriculum Improvement Policy for the *whole* school, what should these secondary senior leaders be trying to achieve?

THE AIMS OF THE CURRICULUM IMPROVEMENT POLICY

The aims of the policy are:

- to increase the use of diagnostic self-evaluation in promoting change that drives up standards of student achievement and attainment;
- to gather reliable evidence of, and make judgements about, the curriculum work that is taking place within the school to inform school self-evaluation;
- to identify good practice and to disseminate this throughout the school;
- to identify poor practice and to formulate a plan of action to improve it;
- to take note of student opinion in order to make the school a better place for them to be and to help them to make more progress;
- to inform future planning and actions in driving up standards (school and department development planning, Continuing Professional Development).

In order to achieve these aims, senior leaders themselves will need to engage directly in Quality Assurance and there is no getting away from the need for them to be overtly inspectorial to achieve this.

The SLT will need to devise a programme of 'inspections' or MERs at the beginning of the academic year, each MER with a leader and an inspection team drawn from their own ranks. This programme will be known only to them and will be made known to the subject or faculty leader to be 'MERed' just two or three days in advance of the MER itself.

Each 'inspection' or MER will:

- last up to five school days, depending on the size of the department or faculty or on the focus of the 'inspection';
- involve the 'inspection team leader' filling out agreed reports that use the standard headings indicated later; these headings will be known in advance to the subject or faculty leader;

- include lesson observations (unannounced), again with a 'known' pro forma (see Appendix 2, pp. 137–8), structured discussion with students and an interview with the head of department or faculty leader;
- conclude with formal written feedback and a discussion involving the inspection team leader, the faculty leader or head of department and the head teacher. This 'feedback' will itself conclude with a list of action points with time-frame. This list will be the focus of the next MER which will usually be during the next academic year – should areas of real concern be identified, the time-frames will reduce as will the gap between this and the next MER which could be that same academic year, or even, in some extreme cases, that same term.

Examples of actual written feedback documents follow and you will notice that the concept of 'ranking' is in operation with each section within each MER, and the MER itself, being judged and wrapped up into a one word, Ofsted category.

Some would argue that it is heavy handed and even destructive, others that it is unambiguous and lucid. Whatever your view, few can claim it to be anything other than:

- on-going;
- focused on learning;
- child-centred;
- challenging.

However, it will be less than constructive, and the twin, linked objectives of enhanced student learning and enhanced student progress will not be achieved, if the ethos and atmosphere throughout the whole school, and in particular throughout the MER process, is not '**low fear**'.

There are those who would claim this to be *the* central and most important point of all and it has certainly been my experience that those being led are in fact happy and content to receive direction from those being paid to shoulder that responsibility. The troops are not in a power struggle with the officers. I would go so far as to say that teachers and students tend not to care about what their leaders know, as long as they know that their leaders care, and they (teachers and students) are more than happy to be led as long as they feel 'valued'. To be 'inspectorial' is therefore far from controversial; it is expected. The essential question thus becomes:

> ### How do senior leaders create/generate/fashion/make available a low-fear environment?

If the reader remembers just one thing from this book I hope that it would be that **senior leaders cannot create a low-fear environment by talking about it.**

Those being led will recognise it when they see it, they will know they are being valued without being told because they will feel it, an atmosphere or environment 'is' it is not 'discussed' or 'described' or 'explained'; it 'is'.

So, senior leaders should adopt and celebrate the Michael Fullan approach to managing change as they strive to create that low-fear environment: talk about it very little if at all especially at the beginning, get on with it and move at pace, and modify if, as and when appropriate.

The low-fear environment needs to exist before awareness of it can happen. The troops need to see it in action so that their conscious awareness can and will be followed by unconscious awareness – when this happens it is, for the senior leader, job done.

Only when the reality of a department or faculty MER is know to those being MERed; only when middle leaders and classroom teachers are *shown* by actual practice that senior leaders are out to support them and that the head teacher is not looking for evidence to get rid of them, will they truly espouse and champion the process that is monitoring, evaluating and reviewing. Only then will it truly become a process done *with* and not done *to*.

An example of a formal feedback document for an English faculty is shown on p. 104.

ENGLISH MER

Achievement and standards

Key Stage 3: *Satisfactory (confirms departmental judgement)*

Results at Key Stage 3 dipped from 82% level 5+ in 2006 to 77% in 2007 and failed to hit the target of 85%. Targets of 50% Level 6+ and 10% level 7 were set; the actual results being 31% and 7% respectively. The percentage of students making progress of two levels from KS2–KS3 has dropped from 79% to 60%. This is against the trend that has seen a steady increase from 2004–2006 inclusive.

3.45% of the G&T cohort performed 1.5–1 level lower than Fischer (FFT) D and 10.34% were 0.5 to 1 level lower.

The Contextual Value Added (CVA) for KS2–3 is not available at this time.

These results are significantly lower than those for maths and science.

Key Stage 4: *Satisfactory (confirms departmental judgement)*

At Key Stage 4 the percentage of students achieving 5A*–C in English of 61.7% was in line with FFT D but significantly below the school targets and results in the other core subjects. This significantly affected the school's capped 5 A*–C which was 20% below the 5 A*–C uncapped.

A*–C in English literature was 68.9% again in line with FFT D but below the school target.

53.1% of boys achieved a C or above in English; 69.7% of girls. This gender difference was not apparent in maths or science.

63.3% of the G&T cohort performed lower than their Fischer D target (53.9% in the LEA), none performed higher than Fischer.

The KS 2–4 CVA in English has dropped from 1002 in 2004 to 999.7 in 2007 placing it in the 57th percentile.

Key Stage 5

English language: *Satisfactory*

English literature: *Inadequate*

(Confirms departmental judgement)

English language

AS   −1   residual against school targets. ALPS 8

A2   0   residual against school targets. ALPS 4
                 (last year 7)

English literature

AS   −1.72   residual against school targets. ALPS 8

A2   −0.22   against ALPS. ALPS 6

Pupil attitudes and behaviour

Key Stage 3: *Satisfactory* *(challenges departmental judgement of good)*

Ten students were interviewed: four Y7; three Y8 and three Y9. Three students said that they enjoyed lessons; two said they enjoyed it sometimes with the remainder saying that it was 'boring'. In all years students claimed that the work was easy and needed to be more challenging and three linked their relatively bad behaviour to 'being bored'.

In the lessons observed there was significant low-level disruption which went unchallenged, there were also students off task.

Key Stage 4: *Satisfactory* *(challenges departmental judgement of good)*

Five students were interviewed. Three said that they enjoyed lessons whilst the remaining two did not like the subject. One Y10 and one Y11 student claimed that the work was too easy and they would appreciate more challenge in lessons. Behaviour in lessons was not an issue for any of the students.

In the lessons observed there were students off task due to a lack of pace and challenge and there was evidence of students not listening to other students when required to do so.

Key Stage 5: *Good (improves on departmental judgement of satisfactory)*

Seven students were interviewed, all except one, said that, on the whole, they enjoyed the lessons. Six said that the work was suitably challenging and that they were well supported in completing it; one Y12 literature student however, finds the work too easy. They all felt behaviour was good in lessons and that everyone was on task for the majority of the lesson.

In the lessons observed students displayed positive attitudes towards learning and teacher–student relationships were good.

Teaching and learning

Key Stage 3: *Satisfactory (challenges the departmental judgement of good with elements of satisfactory)*

Seven lessons were observed: two Y7, one Y8, three Y9, two were judged inadequate, three satisfactory and two good. There was an absence of observable planning for lessons but, in the two good lessons, the lesson plans were detailed and aided learning. The key problem displayed in the lessons was a lack of pace and challenge leading to students lacking engagement. There was also too much tolerance of low-level disruption.

Key Stage 4: *Satisfactory (challenges departmental judgement of good)*

Two lessons were observed: one Y10 and one Y11 both of which were satisfactory. In one lesson learning objectives were not shared with the class, although they did become clear as the lesson progressed. In the Y11 lesson, students were bored which resulted in low-level disruption. The lesson was also characterised by too much teacher-talk leading to a lack of independent learning. Both lessons observed were characterised by a lack of pace and challenge and students did not demonstrate perceptible progress.

Key Stage 5

Literature: *Satisfactory (confirms departmental judgement)*

Language: *Good (improves departmental judgement of satisfactory)*

Three lessons were observed in total: two Y12 (literature and language) and one Y13 language lesson. Two lessons were judged to be satisfactory while the third was outstanding. The satisfactory lessons were characterised by the dominance of teacher-talk and did not give sufficient prominence to independent learning. The didactic style meant there was more focus on teaching than learning.

There is clearly expertise and good practice in this area which needs to be disseminated.

Use of ICT

Key Stage 3: *Satisfactory (confirms departmental judgement)*

In some lessons there was good use of the data projector and reference was made to homework on the VLE (Virtual Learning Environment). Use is made of the laptops in lessons and there is sharing of ICT resources and good practice. Currently, there are no procedures in place to monitor the impact of ICT on teaching and learning but there are plans in place to use student voice to partly address this.

Key Stage 4: *Satisfactory (confirms departmental judgement)*

Data projectors are used for PowerPoint presentations and there is a growing bank of resources including homeworks on the VLE. Use is made of the laptops in lessons and there is sharing of ICT resources and good practice. Currently, there are no procedures in place to monitor the impact of ICT on teaching and learning but there are plans in place to use student voice to partly address this.

Key Stage 5: *Satisfactory (confirms departmental judgement)*

Data projectors are used for PowerPoint presentations and there are some resources including homeworks on the VLE. Use is made of the laptops in lessons and there is sharing of ICT resources and good practice. Currently, there are no procedures in place to monitor the impact of ICT on teaching and learning but there are plans in place to use statistics of VLE usage.

Assessment, recording and reporting

Key Stage 3: *Inadequate* *(challenges departmental judgement of good)*

Only one student, of the ten interviewed, a Y8 student, knew her current attainment level and only two Y8 and one Y9 student could give their end of year target. None of the four Y7 students could give any information about how well they were doing in English. No one could articulate what they needed to do to achieve a specific level or how to improve their work. This was also evident in the majority of observed lessons. In one lesson, however, students could articulate their current and target levels and could show documentation that gave clear targets linked to assessment criteria. In several lessons there was an absence of marking in students' books and students did not take pride in presentation with work exhibiting doodles and scribbling.

Key Stage 4: *Satisfactory* *(challenges departmental judgement of satisfactory with elements of good)*

Of the three Y11 students interviewed, only one had any idea of his current attainment level, but he wasn't sure whether it was an A or an A*; all three knew their target grades. All three Y10 students knew their current attainment grades and their end of year aspirational and likely target grades. None of the KS4 students could articulate what they needed to do to attain their target grades.

In the lessons observed students knew their current attainment and their likely and aspirational targets but could not articulate what they needed to do to improve the standard of their work.

Key Stage 5: *Satisfactory* *(confirms departmental judgement)*

Two out of three Y12 students; two out of four Y13 students knew their current attainment; but all students knew their target grade. None of the Y13 students knew what they had to do to achieve their target grades; all of the Y12 students had a satisfactory grasp of what is required.

In lessons students knew their current attainment and target grades and could, to some degree, articulate what they needed to do to improve.

Leadership and management

Inadequate (*challenges departmental judgement of satisfactory*)

Poor leadership and a lack of Quality Assurance have contributed to the decline in attainment. Although there have been staffing problems, there were also issues with guidance and support of unqualified teachers. Key Stage leaders have not been involved in the self-evaluation process and have been denied opportunities to demonstrate leadership skills due to the dominance of the faculty leader.

The FACULTY LEADER has now put in place a programme for Quality Assurance, which involves Key Stage leaders leading on their Key Stage.

Overall judgement

Satisfactory

Areas for development:

- To improve leadership in the faculty at all key stages.
- To focus upon and implement strategies to narrow the gender gap by improving boys' attainment.
- To dramatically improve Quality Assurance to inform accurate self-evaluation.
- To ensure that data is used accurately to inform targeted intervention.
- To ensure that short-term planning is pertinent to the needs and ability of the class to be taught.
- To ensure that students' work is appropriately assessed and that AFL is integrated into lessons such that students are aware of what they need to do to improve their attainment.
- To ensure that strategies are in place for the sharing of good practice.
- To put strategies in place to ensure that G&T students at least achieve their 'likely' target.

Clearly, the next MER will begin with the areas for development and, while it will follow the prescribed headings, the drive will be the above formal feedback document.

It may be that the SLT has perceived a non-subject specific area of concern for the *whole* school and a non-subject MER might well be called for. An example of a formal feedback document (to be given to the staff as a whole) for this 'type' of MER is as follows:

SIXTH FORM MER

The rationale

Improving teaching and learning in the Sixth Form is a key objective in the school's development plan. In the SEF (self-evaluation form) we have judged ourselves as 'Satisfactory' in this area; this judgement was corroborated by Ofsted earlier this year. According to ALPS we are a 5. The aim of the MER is to identify areas of good practice that can be disseminated to all departments and to identify areas that we must improve if we are to progress towards 'Outstanding' and a 1 in ALPS.

A large percentage of our two days' INSET in January will be devoted to teaching and learning in the Sixth Form and will be informed by the findings of the MER.

The two strands of the MER were lesson observations and student questionnaires.

Lesson observations

Lesson observations were carried out in the following subjects: biology, CACHE, chemistry, drama, English, general studies, history, mathematics, media, PE, physics, psychology, sociology and travel and tourism. Other observations were planned but, due to staff being out of school for a variety of reasons, did not take place.

Good practice

There were examples of outstanding practice and, without fail, these lessons followed the three/four-part structure with the focus very heavily on learning as opposed to teaching.

Good practice was characterised by:

- Thorough **lesson planning**. Planning that included: learning objectives, success criteria, and starter activity, development activity(ies) which fostered independent or group learning, opportunities for AFL, multiple intelligences, differentiation, plenary.
- Good **subject knowledge and a clear enthusiasm** for the subject that was communicated to and rubbed off on the students.
- **Learning objectives** shared with the students, referred to during the lesson and returned to at the end. The use of **learning logs/ tracker sheets in science** in which students recorded the learning objectives and assessed their learning at the end of the lesson were highly effective and **may profitably be used in other subjects**.
- Clear links to and consolidation of **prior learning** – students understood what they were learning and how it fitted in with prior and, on occasion, future learning. Their learning was put in context.

Students demonstrated their prior learning either verbally, in a short learning activity or in a short test.

- Clear **success criteria** – students knew what was expected of them by the end of the lesson.
- Students were engaged in their own learning – the vast majority of the lessons were devoted to students **using and developing their skills for independent learning**: working in pairs, groups or individually on a learning activity. The balance between teacher-talk and student learning was very heavily loaded towards the latter.
- In the best lessons the teacher input focused on **modelling** or **AFL**.
- Teachers provided **targeted support** for students who needed stretching or who needed help.
- In **group work** all students had a clear role and knew what they had to produce by the end of the activity.
- Where needed, learning activities were **differentiated**.
- Students were encouraged to use a variety of **Intelligences** to solve problems or to demonstrate learning.

- **AFL** was used so that students were able to assess **their own learning** – giving themselves an attainment grade and identifying what they needed to do to achieve the higher grade.
- **Questioning** was challenging and instrumental in helping students to clarify and articulate their learning. Questions were open and directed at specific students, thinking time was built in, and answers were challenged and passed on to others for developing.
- The lesson ended with a **plenary** which returned to the objectives and success criteria. All students were involved in the plenary and could explain what they had learnt. By the end of the lesson it was clear that **students had made progress**.

Areas for improvement

After every lesson the observed teacher received feedback and areas for development were discussed with the observer. There was the occasional lesson in which learning objectives were not evident and a few that did not have a plenary but these were very much in the minority. **All teachers are aware of the school policy for lesson planning and their reasons for not following school policy were discussed in the de-brief**. There is no benefit, therefore, in listing all the examples where school policy was not observed, or in highlighting areas for improvement which are specific to individual lessons and have already been discussed at an individual level.

There is, however, a need for heads of departments and faculty leaders to check lesson planning to ensure that it adheres to school policy by including: lesson objectives, success criteria, starter activity, development activities focused on independent learning, differentiation, and a plenary. Heads of departments and faculty leaders also need to have systems in place to monitor that the plans are adhered to in practice.

The following areas were identified in a significant number of lessons and are considered to be important in the future development of teaching and learning in the Sixth Form.

Prompt start to lessons

A significant number of students were late for lessons and teachers waited for their arrival.

Action to be taken

- The Sixth Form team to address this issue in assembly and form periods.
- Teachers to start lessons promptly – late comers should not be waited for and lessons should not be disturbed by their late arrival.
- All students who are late should be spoken to **at the end of the lesson**, made to explain the reason for their lateness and warned that a cause for concern slip will be sent the next time they are late.

Too much teacher-talk – balance in favour of teaching rather than learning

Examples of this were:

- Teacher telling the students what they had previously learnt – students should tell the teacher or demonstrate prior learning in a short activity or test.
- The teacher explaining what students had to do in great detail when the instructions were already prepared in writing for students to follow. Students could have read them and then explained to the teacher what they had to do, or could have started the activity using the instructions.
- Closed questions being asked and the teacher then elaborating on or developing the answer further – students being told the teacher's opinion before being allowed to form their own.
- Notes being copied or dictated – students need to engage with the text by making and personalising their own notes.
- Watching a video and then the teacher telling students what they should have learnt from it.
- The plenary being done by the teacher – i.e. students are told what they should have learned rather than students demonstrating what they have learned.

Action to be taken

- To be addressed in January INSET.
- To be addressed by the teaching and learning team and coaching.

Lack of structure and purpose in group work

In some lessons, students were told to discuss things in groups but did not have the skills for effective group work. Clear roles were not assigned to group members and there was no specific purpose or outcome given.

This has been identified as an area of concern in KS3 and KS4 through the MER and student shadowing.

Action to be taken
- To be addressed in January INSET.
- To be addressed by the teaching and learning team and coaching.

Differentiation

This was seen as an issue in groups where the spread of ability was particularly wide and neither the higher-ability nor lower-ability students were catered for. Learning objectives, success criteria and learning activities were not differentiated.

This has also been identified as an area of concern in KS3 and KS4 through the MER.

Action to be taken
- To be addressed in January INSET.
- To be addressed by teaching and learning team and coaching.

Assessment for learning

There was evidence of students not understanding the assessment criteria or of not being able to apply them in peer or self-assessment.

Action to be taken
- The response from student questionnaires needs to be analysed with respect to AFL before the nature of future action is decided. It is likely, however, that this will be done at departmental level with advice and monitoring provided by the director of learning.

Lack of structure and purpose in coursework lessons

In coursework lessons students were left to 'get on' without clear expectations or outcomes being set.

Action to be taken

- This will be tackled at departmental level in the departments identified by the MER, but it is mentioned here as it may be current practice in other subjects when coursework is undertaken in lessons. It is therefore, necessary for heads of departments and faculty leaders to ensure that coursework lessons are structured and there are clear learning outcomes for all students.

Insufficient use being made of multiple intelligences

Some lessons relied solely on verbal-linguistic learning and in most lessons students demonstrated learning in writing.

Action to be taken

- To be addressed in January INSET.

The way forward

1 **Good practice** identified in the report to be disseminated to staff either by:
   - whole staff briefing in the hall after school
   - discussion at faculty leaders group and taken back to faculties.
   - the faculty leader for science explaining the use of learning logs and tracker sheets in science with faculty leaders at faculty leaders group.

2 **Punctual arrival at lessons** to be addressed as outlined above.

3 **Lack of structure** in coursework lessons to be discussed by the director of learning with the teachers and departments concerned.

4 **AFL**
   - The director of learning to conduct an audit of AFL in the Sixth Form.
   - The director of learning to identify areas for improvement and to work with faculty leaders and heads of departments to improve AFL.

5 **INSET** – to focus on:
   - independent learning
   - group work
   - differentiation
   - multiple intelligences.

Planning needs to begin immediately for the INSET; the video approach in our last INSET was particularly successful and we would like to video some lessons to be used in the INSET. This would focus on **deliberate** bad practice as well as good practice. Many of the areas above, if not all, could be focused upon in this way.

A video of students giving their views on how they best learn could be used – this was successful in the AFL INSET.

We could also look at lesson plans to identify good and not so good practice.

Group work could be approached by demonstrating different techniques with staff.

Differentiation could be covered in a formal presentation on different approaches to differentiation.

6 Coaching

- The faculty leader for science and the director of learning to work with faculty leaders and heads of departments to identify outstanding Sixth Form teachers and teachers in need of support to develop their practice.

- The outstanding teachers would form a Sixth Form teaching and learning (TAL) team and would be further trained as coaches by the faculty leader for science and the director of learning.

- The coaches would be paired with teachers in need of coaching.

- Monitoring, evaluating and reviewing of the process to be led by the faculty leader for science and the director of learning.

No doubt you can see from the detail involved in these actual examples that this is a tremendous time and work commitment for members of the SLT. I would argue nevertheless that it is a commitment that they cannot afford to shun. Indeed it would be difficult for any senior leader to play down the importance, and centrality, of Quality Assurance to their role.

Regrettably some senior leaders have no real view on Quality Assurance and their part in it because they have not thought through their role and their priorities. They turn up each day, react to what happens and leave happy that they have worked hard. They have no notion of being 'watched'. As a young teacher, I was advised many times by one more-senior colleague to 'always work on your own credibility son; it's not who you are but how you are perceived that counts'.

Whether we like it or not, we teachers are 'known' by many more people than we know, and often our character is invented and then described to others by children; these others then have an annoying habit of forming indiscriminate opinions about us. This is even more true about senior leaders who are ruthlessly pigeonholed by children, parents, governors and by those professionals that they lead; and this labelling is far more about what they do and the evidence of what they do than it is concerned with what they say.

An SLT that overtly prioritises and is personally involved in on-going monitoring, evaluation and review can only be a team that believes in learning and in the raising of student achievement. The onus is then on any other individual involved or simply 'watching' – teacher, parent, governor, child, LEA personnel – to dispute and discredit this. When the MER process is as high profile and thorough as shown above, any gainsayer will have their work cut out.

However, the low-fear environment is key and even a casual reading of the examples above of formal feedback documents will show that there is a danger that they will appear, and therefore that they will be, threatening.

Senior leaders that value their workforce are naturally inclined to involve that workforce and their natural leadership style is open. It is difficult, I would say impossible, to appear to value a workforce that is kept in the dark. So the questions for which answers are sought should not be pulled firmly to the collective senior leadership chest. Senior leaders should not regress to their primary school days when they (and didn't we all) kept our non-writing arm wrapped around our unique and innovative work for fear that the nine-year-old at the next desk might steal our pearls of wisdom. Like speed cameras, the desired outcome in our schools is well known so why hide the device?

Clearly then faculty leaders and heads of department are entitled to a clear and explicit 'heads up' about what is expected of them, so the faculty leader/head of department will be given the following (see also Quality Assurance procedures – guidance for subject leaders – Appendix 4, pp. 140–2) as well as as many opportunities to discuss it with senior leaders as they feel that they need:

1 Subject/faculty leaders will be required to complete a subject self-evaluation document at the beginning of each school year. This is a working document to be revisited periodically and updated immediately prior to the commencement of MER.
2 Subject/faculty leaders will be required to engage in a formal, on-going Quality Assurance process throughout the year.
3 Subject/faculty leaders will meet with their line manager once per half term to review progress and focus on school improvement. This model should also be used by faculty leaders in line-managing their subject leaders and Key Stage coordinators.
4 The SLT may use a range of strategies to evaluate and support the effectiveness of departments and identify whole-school priorities and training needs, including:

- review meetings with subject/faculty leaders;
- cross-curricular audits;
- student interviews/questionnaires;
- shadowing;
- lesson observations (see Appendices 1, 2 and 3, pp. 136–9);
- formal MER (see below).

What follows is a clear 'blow-by-blow' account of what the faculty/department leader can expect and what is expected of them from a formal MER.

FORMAL MER

Curriculum monitoring, evaluation and review will take place throughout the year and need not be triggered by any particular senior leadership concerns.

All MER will be conducted as follows:

- The faculty/subject leader will be given two or three school days' notice.
- The faculty/subject leader will be expected to ensure that an updated self-evaluation form (SEF) is available to the senior leader heading the MER team by the first day of the MER.
- The faculty/subject leader will be asked to meet with the MER leader at the start of the MER period. There will be a need, at this meeting, for the faculty/subject leader to more fully explain the subject SEF and to produce Quality Assurance evidence.
- The MER team will scrutinise pupil attainment data and compare to Section 1 of the subject SEF.
- Members of the MER team will observe a sample of lessons, making judgements using Ofsted criteria. Formative feedback will be given using the school's lesson observation sheet.
- Members of the MER team will interview a sample of students.
- Members of the MER team may scrutinise pupils' work.
- The faculty/subject leader may be asked to provide copies of schemes of work and any other relevant documentation.
- At the end of the period of the MER a short report will be published. It will contain an overall judgement about the quality of the work being undertaken within the department/faculty as well as judgements about specific aspects. The emphasis will be on the *impact* on student learning and thus on student achievement and attainment.
- The report will inform the agenda of a meeting between the faculty/subject leader, the head teacher, the MER leader and relevant members of the SLT.
- The outcome (list of action points) of this meeting will form the basis of a Curriculum Improvement Plan that must be fed into the Department/Faculty Development Plan, which the subject leader will amend within one week of receiving the MER report.

Given that the SLT will need to share out the 'inspections' between them but that there is a need for uniformity, there should be a 'guide' for them to follow; this will also help in their subsequent planning discussions. This also should be 'shared' with the faculty/department staff.

An example of such a 'guide' is shown below:

MONITORING THE EFFECTIVENESS OF THE FACULTY OR DEPARTMENT

The following is a model for use by the SLT and faculty leaders, and for faculty leaders to use with their subject leaders or Key Stage coordinators.

What does the line manager need to know about the subject?

- What is the course structure/weighting of exam/coursework?
- Deadlines?
- What are the issues for the department/faculty in terms of performance? How can the leader support, evaluate and challenge actions to bring about improvement?
- What is being done to support inexperienced staff, in particular what support is being given to their teaching of exam groups?
- Do the coursework tasks chosen match the requirements for producing good results? Who can offer support/advice?
- What is done to redraft/improve underperformance in coursework?
- Does the department spend a proportional amount of time on coursework/exam prep?

Reviewing the subject self-evaluation form

1   **Achievement and standards**
    This should be checked for accuracy. The data and its implications have been discussed at meetings such as the residuals meetings. Discuss progress on the action points from the residuals meetings. How good is the faculty or subject leader's evaluation of the previous year's performance?

Follow-up: student monitoring and intervention

- Faculty/subject leader's view on the progress towards and the targets set for each year group?
- Can the faculty/subject leader produce a rank order or an approximation of a rank order of students in each year group?
- Can the faculty/subject leader identify target groups based on data and target intervention where most impact can be made?
- What strategies are in place to support intervention – parental contact, etc.?
- How is the effectiveness of intervention measured?

2 **Pupil attitudes and behaviour**
- What evidence does the faculty/subject leader have of pupils' views on the subject? How are their views gathered?
- What action is taken in response to this?
- What is the level of motivation and engagement in lessons?
- How does the department/faculty respond to behaviour issues?
- How are parents kept informed of curriculum, support, deadlines, problems, etc.?
- How does the faculty use the internet/student intranet for support and communication?

3 **Teaching and learning**
- Discuss the faculty/subject leader's judgements and the evidence for these judgements – are the judgements well informed?
- What are the key factors for improving teaching and learning in the subject or the faculty? How are these being addressed?
- What should we expect to see in lesson observations to show that the areas for development are being addressed?

Follow-up
- Review recent observations.
- What training needs have been identified?
- How is the department addressing these?
- What systems are in place to disseminate good practice?

4 **Use of ICT**
- Does the faculty/subject leader have a considered view/policy on the effective use of ICT within the department or faculty?

- Do lesson plans and schemes of work take into account opportunities to use ICT to improve learning?
- Are views shared and good ICT practice disseminated among faculty/ department members?

Follow-up
- What are the resource implications for the faculty/department in terms of the effective use of ICT?

5 **Assessment, recording and reporting**
- Discuss the judgements and the evidence for them.
- Are the judgements well informed?
- Where can we see good practice with regard to AFL?

Follow-up: AFL focus
- How good is the department's focus on exam performance?
- Are the principles of AFL embedded in their everyday practice?
- What happens after key assessments? (Y10 exams/Y11 'mocks')
- How rigorous are the 'mocks'? Are they a reliable indicator of future performance?
- Has the faculty/department analysed the exam performance to identify the key areas for improvement? What are they doing about it?

6 **Leadership and management**
- How is the leader monitoring the overall quality of leadership and management of the faculty/department?
- Leadership: vision and direction, pace, strategic planning, ability to prioritise, creation of an effective team, focus on raising attainment and improving teaching and learning.
- Staff development, including developing capacity within the team, identifying training needs and potential coaches, support and induction for new and temporary staff.
- Self-evaluation and review, including: exam performance, deployment of staff, and quality of Assessment Recording Reporting.
- Quality and effectiveness of: data analysis, development plans and planning, target setting and intervention, and Quality Assurance evidence.
- Deployment of resources.

7 **Overall effectiveness of the faculty/department**

- Has the leader got an accurate feel for the faculty/department's work?
- Observed lessons, pupil work scrutiny, student interviews and 'spot-check' on application of school policies within the faculty/ department: the setting of learning objectives, classroom climate and discipline, etc. What do the judgements/opinions indicate?
- Conclusions drawn about faculty/department planning and preparation and the review the Faculty/Subject Development Plan.

Clearly, MER is not simply confined to faculties and departments and the year teams should have their own MER. An example of a Pastoral Self-evaluation Form can be found on pp. 124–31.

The classroom teacher and other managers and leaders in primary and secondary schools can modify much of this to facilitate self-MER and MER of the progress of students. The principles and processes of MER are adaptable and applicable to most situations and circumstances.

As time progresses and the MER process becomes more embedded, it will become more self-driven and less inspectorial. The MER 'team' will and should begin to involve middle as well as senior managers, and then staff with no management responsibilities and NQTs. In this way the objective to spread good practice and to cross-fertilise good ideas will be facilitated and enhanced.

However, the summative need to know must not be sacrificed to the formative need to grow and senior leaders must be prepared to halt proceedings every now and again to check the compass. Whole-school direction checking is a senior leader duty and responsibility and these people can never be just a regular member of the gathering. Nobody wants to arrive in London ahead of schedule and feeling good when the destination of choice was Birmingham. If they do, their feeling of achievement will soon dissolve into one of irritation and frustration and they will not hesitate, quite rightly, to blame the driver.

PASTORAL SELF-EVALUATION

Year group _____   *Last updated* _____

Please indicate the SEF judgements as described in this document:

Leadership and management	Pupil attitudes and behaviour	Form period	Assembly	Overall effectiveness of year team

Summarise the strengths and weaknesses of the year team

Action points

1 Leadership and management (head of year)

Outstanding

The head of year has a very good grasp of the data and can describe accurately realistic targets; the head of year can produce a rank order of tutors and show how weaknesses are being addressed; data is used to identify under-performing students, regular homework checks are done and the data is analysed and appropriate action taken; Pastoral Support Plans are in place and are bringing about improvements; the quality of reviews is monitored in a meaningful way; patterns of attendance are monitored and the head of year works with the Education Welfare Officer (EWO) to address problems effectively; the head of year has a timely and visionary plan to improve the performance of the team.

Good

The head of year has a good grasp of the data and can describe accurately realistic targets; the head of year can produce a rank order of tutors; data is used to identify under-performing students, regular homework checks are done and the data is analysed; Pastoral Support Plans are in place and are bringing about some improvements; the quality of reviews is monitored, patterns of attendance are monitored and the head of year works with the EWO to address problems; the head of year has a timely plan to improve the performance of the team.

Satisfactory

The head of year has a fair grasp of the data and can describe realistic targets; the head of year can produce a rank order of tutors; data is used to identify under-performing students, homework checks are done and the data is analysed; Pastoral Support Plans are in place; the quality of reviews is monitored; patterns of attendance are monitored and the head of year works with the EWO to address problems; the head of year has a plan to improve the performance of the team.

Inadequate

The head of year has little grasp of the data and cannot describe realistic targets; the head of year can produce a rank order of tutors but it is not based on meaningful evidence; data is seldom used to identify under-performing students; homework checks are done but no analysis is done with the data; Pastoral Support Plans are in place; the quality of reviews is rarely monitored; patterns of attendance are monitored but the head of year does not work with the EWO to address problems; the head of year has no plan to improve the performance of the team.

Questions to consider

- Can you as head of year describe statistically where the cohort should be by the end of the year in terms of GCSE grades or NC levels?
- Can you identify high-performing and weak tutors? What is the evidence basis for this?

- Can you identify a number of under-performing students? What is this judgement based on?
- Do you know which curriculum areas set homework and which do not? What action have they taken to address this?
- Do you know who has a Pastoral Support Plan? How do you know if the plan is making a difference?
- Do you have evidence of your own monitoring, evaluation and reviews for your year team?
- What support do you give to NQTs?
- Can you identify patterns of absence in the year group and do you know who the persistent latecomers are? What have you done to address the problem?
- Have you got a good grasp of how to bring about further improvements in student performance?
- Do you have specific plans or programmes specific to the year group?
- Can you provide the most recent Pastoral Improvement Plan and evidence progress towards targets?

Self-evaluation grade

Grade	Evidence

2 Pupil attitudes and behaviour

Outstanding

Students are very confident that bullying is dealt with firmly and fairly. They feel very safe. Students see form period as a valuable learning opportunity. The students have a very good grasp on their current attainment levels and can describe their targets accurately. Students know where else to turn to for support and feel that the school has their interests at heart. The students take every opportunity of the extra-curricular activities available. The students are able to describe a range of high-quality, work-related learning activities. The students are very confident in expressing their views and feel that they are taken seriously. The head of year has clear systems in place to gather student opinion and modifies priorities accordingly.

Good

Students are confident that bullying is dealt with firmly and fairly. They feel safe. Students sometimes see form period as a valuable learning opportunity. The students have a fair grasp on their current attainment levels and can describe their targets accurately. Students have some idea of where else to turn to for support and feel that the school has their interests at heart. The students take opportunity of the extra-curricular activities available. The students are able to describe a range of work-related learning activities. The students are confident in expressing their views and feel that they are taken seriously. The head of year has sound systems in place to gather student opinion and modifies priorities.

Satisfactory

Students are confident that bullying is dealt with. They feel safe. Students sometimes see form period as a learning opportunity. The students have a limited grasp on their current attainment levels and can describe their targets. Students have some idea of where else to turn to for support and feel that the school has their interests at heart. The students sometimes take opportunity of the extra-curricular activities available. The students are able to describe a work-related learning activity. The students are confident in expressing their views and feel that they are taken seriously. The head of year has some systems in place to gather student opinion.

Inadequate

Students are not confident that bullying is dealt with. They feel unsafe at times. Students seldom see form period as a learning opportunity. The students have a limited grasp on their current attainment levels and cannot describe their targets. Students have some idea of where else to turn to for support but feel that the school does not have their interests at heart. The students seldom take opportunity of the extra-curricular activities available. The students are not able to describe a work-related learning activity. The students are not confident in expressing their views and feel that they are not taken seriously. The head of year does not have systems in place to gather student opinion and year group priorities are not informed by student voice.

Questions to consider

- Do you feel that incidents of bullying are dealt with quickly and satisfactorily?
- Do students value what happens in form period? How do you know?
- Can the majority of students tell you what their targets are and how to achieve them? How do you monitor target setting?
- What percentage of students has contact with outside agencies? How valuable is this contact?
- Do the majority of students have access to extra-curricular activities?
- Do students feel confident in expressing their views about the school?
- Do the students feel that the school listens to them?
- What systems do you have in place for gathering student views?
- How does student voice affect your priorities as a head of year?

Self-evaluation grade

Grade	Evidence

3 Form period

Outstanding

The register is routinely 100% accurate; form period activities are taking place according to an agreed timetable; tutors have a positive and professional relationship with the class; messages are dealt with clearly and efficiently; students almost without exception know their potential and current level of attainment, almost all students can describe what they need to do to improve, planners are flawless. Other adults/prefects are very well deployed.

Good

The register is routinely 100% accurate; tutors have a positive relationship with the group; messages are given out; form period activities take place and most students understand what they are for; most students can tell you what their potential is and know where they fall short currently, planners are well used. Other adults/prefects are well deployed.

Satisfactory

The register is routinely 100% accurate; the relationship between tutors and their class is sound; messages are given out; form period activities are completed but not all students are able to explain why they take place; students know their potential but are not sure how to go about improving, planners have gaps but are being used and checked. Other adults/prefects are deployed but make little impact.

Inadequate

The register is not routinely accurate; the relationship is strained; messages are not given out; form period activities rarely happen and students do not understand why they happen; students do not know their potential and have little or no idea about how to improve, planners are poorly used and seldom checked. Other adults/prefects make little or no difference to form period.

Questions to consider

Does the teacher:
- complete an accurate register?
- know the students' names?
- engage students in positive interaction?
- give messages where relevant?
- ensure that planned activities are completed (Learn to Learn, Progress File, Citizenship, Inter-form etc.)?
- encourage a positive atmosphere in form period?

Questions to consider regarding students in the year group:
- Can students tell you what their targets are?
- Do students know how to achieve their targets?
- Do students know how the bullying policy works?
- Are the systems for managing behaviour effective?
- Are planners signed by parents and teachers?
- Is homework being recorded on a regular basis?

Self-evaluation grade

Grade   Evidence

4 Assembly

Outstanding
Assemblies routinely provide a high level of challenge. They are thought provoking, encourage a great deal of personal reflection, and there is good evidence of spiritual/moral/social content. The whole process is always well ordered.

Good
There is a good level of challenge, with some opportunity for personal reflection, evidence of S/M/S content, undertaken in reasonable order.

Satisfactory
The assembly engages the attention of the students and there is some reflection but this is limited. There is some S/M/S content, but this is limited. Order is maintained but there may be some distractions.

Inadequate
There is minimal challenge in assemblies, and there is little or no opportunity for personal reflection. S/M/S links are not made explicit, and order is not always maintained.

Questions to consider

On a week to week basis:
- Do students arrive in an orderly manner?
- Are the students smart in their appearance?
- Is the input creative and thought provoking?
- Are the students given the chance to reflect?
- Do the students listen attentively?
- Do assemblies incorporate social, moral and cultural dimensions?
- Do assemblies encourage a shared year group/school identity?
- Do assemblies motivate students to greater achievement and attainment?

Self-evaluation grade

Grade	*Evidence*

5 Overall effectiveness of year-group team

As a team, consider your responses to the four areas of this self-evaluation, and place the team in one of the four categories:

Outstanding   Good   Satisfactory   or   Inadequate

Overall effectiveness of the year group team – self-evaluation rating

Comments:

8

SUMMARY

All good lessons have a list of key words to remember and to define the lesson, and what follows is an attempt to distil the key words from the preceding pages:

1 **Lead** – The head teacher more than anybody leads the school, but leadership should be found throughout the school, and all adults working in the school should apply leadership throughout the day. Leadership requires vision (good leaders regularly write 'position papers' or articulate their 'vision' for others to constructively criticise), commitment, determination and drive. Good leaders are brave and single-minded; they take calculated risks and they have a sense of urgency. Good schools and classrooms are led by individuals not committees.

2 **Discipline** – A high-challenge/low-fear environment must always be in evidence, and the school should be characterised by a calm and business-like atmosphere. The SLT and, in particular, the head teacher, is the focus for that discipline, and no student can be allowed to disrupt the learning of others.

3 **Learning** – Learning is the central purpose of all schools, and a clear and shared understanding of exactly what this means

is essential. Good schools do not become involved in the myriad ideas and initiatives that do not involve learning. A clear understanding of learning as an activity is essential, as is the total involvement of the learner.

4   **Systems** – Most schools are large institutions and a commitment to clear, simple and understandable systems will enable all to focus on the core purpose of learning.

5   **Contrast, compare and communicate** – Teachers have no real idea of whether learning has taken place unless they continuously collect and use data formatively. They must use the data to contrast and compare (residuals and ranking) and this is of central importance. Senior leaders should insist upon the data being quickly collected and collated, simply and understandably documented and, most importantly, communicated to as wide a circle of interested parties as possible. Examples of the kind of data required are:

- a student's performance in one subject compared with the same student's performance in another subject;
- a group or cohort's performance in one subject compared with the same group or cohort's performance in another subject;
- the school's performance compared to other schools;
- student effort, etc.

6   **Outcomes** – There is a good deal of misunderstanding and, in some cases, hypocrisy around educational outcomes. People who care passionately about outcomes for their own children, seem – apparently – less passionate about outcomes for other people's children. League tables are good if you're a parent, and they should be good if you're a teacher. We can agree that examinations are not totally accurate, and that league tables can mislead, but the self-indulgent conference culture that often replaces a real critique of what we are actually going to do to improve, is no solution; a determination to discuss and debate the rules of the game may well be interesting, but it will be futile, unless you like losing. The game is what it is: get on with it!

Outstanding senior leaders pursue outcomes relentlessly and unambiguously – these leaders are not content until they have 'closed the deal'.

7 **Student centred** – Good schools involve students in their own learning process and not just because it is 'fair'. Good schools understand that it is a student's responsibility (it's their job) to know their current academic level in any particular subject, to know what this means, to know what is involved in progressing to the next level and to know what they have to do to make that improvement. Just as importantly, the student needs to know the time frame and resources involved.

8 **Pace** – Justice delayed is justice denied, and good schools and good teachers are fully aware of the need to maintain a rapid pace if they are to reduce student underachievement to a minimum. The tendency in schools to plan for things to happen 'next year' should be challenged. Teachers have the students in front of them for only 25 hours per week, and 38 weeks per year, and they have a duty to know to the minute whether they are using that time as wisely and as well as they could. A sense of urgency is a prerequisite for good teaching and good schools.

9 **Change** – Change is to be welcomed and managed and where possible step change is desirable since it is often much more effective than the staged variety. Individuals, organisations, groups etc. can go forward or they can go back. There is no third alternative.

10 **High expectations** – Always!

APPENDICES

LESSON OBSERVATION PRINCIPLES AND PROCESS

PRINCIPLES

- Lesson observation must focus on learning – not what the teacher does.
- The focus must be on the students – what are they learning?
- There must be a clear understanding of what success looks like.
- The observation must take teaching and learning forward.
- It must be a positive experience for all involved.

PROCESS

- If the observation is to be 'announced' (known about in advance of the observation by the teacher to be observed), there must be a pre-observation meeting in which the lesson plan is given to the observer and the success criteria are shared with the observer; this clearly would be inappropriate if the observation is to be unannounced as it would be as part of a MER.
- The observer must arrive at the lesson promptly and stay, unless otherwise agreed, for the full lesson.
- The observation must be recorded on the school's observation pro forma (see Appendix 2).
- There must be a post-observation meeting to discuss the observation.

OUTCOME

- A copy of the observation form should be given to the teacher and a copy retained by the team leader.

LESSON OBSERVATION PRO FORMA

Subject: ....

Class: .... Date: ....

Teacher: .... Observer: ....

Purpose of observation:

☐ Performance Management
☐ MER
☐ Quality Assurance
☐ NQT
☐ CPD
☐ Other ....

Agreed focus of observation (if applicable):

....

....

....

☐ Lesson plan *(please attach a copy)*
☐ Objectives
☐ Differentiation
☐ Multiple intelligences
☐ Plenary

Desired outcome Yes/No	**Needs identified and met Yes/No**
• Learning put in context	• SEN students on code of practice
• Engagement	• Gifted & Talented students
• Challenge and support	• Middle ability students
• Independent learning	
• Assessment for learning	
• Perceptible progress	

Teaching	**Learning**
What the teacher does to facilitate learning:	What students do to demonstrate learning:

LESSON OBSERVATION PRO FORMA *(continued)*

Lesson observation feedback

Positive features of the lesson   Areas for improvement

```
┌─────────────────────────────────────┐
│                                     │
│                                     │
│                                     │
│                                     │
└─────────────────────────────────────┘
```

Ofsted judgement

Targets for improvement   **Possible strategies**

```
┌─────────────────────────────────────┐
│                                     │
│                                     │
│                                     │
│                                     │
└─────────────────────────────────────┘
```

Teacher reflection on evaluation of the lesson

```
┌─────────────────────────────────────┐
│                                     │
│                                     │
│                                     │
│                                     │
└─────────────────────────────────────┘
```

Future observation planned? Yes / No

Agreed focus:

```
┌─────────────────────────────────────┐
│                                     │
│                                     │
│                                     │
│                                     │
└─────────────────────────────────────┘
```

Signature of teacher ....
Date: ....

Signature of observer ....
Date: ....

LESSON OBSERVATION: GUIDANCE FOR OBSERVERS

What to look for	What to look for
Objectives – Measurable, linked to prior learning, clearly expressed – Pupils can describe what they are expected to learn and how they will be assessed	**AFL** – Awareness of pupil data – Formative oral and written feedback – Teacher shows detailed knowledge of level/grade descriptors and encourages awareness in pupils – Peer and self-assessment – Pupils know what to do to access the next level/grade – On-going assessment throughout lesson
Starter activity – Resources prepared – Pupils engaged and on task quickly – Activity stimulates curiosity/interest – Element of challenge?	**Homework** – Previous non-doers challenged – Clear purpose, clearly explained – Appropriate level of challenge
Main body of lesson – Awareness of multiple intelligences – Appropriate balance of strategies and activities (VAK) – Smooth transitions – Pace/timing/chunking – Questioning – ICT	**Classroom management** – Orderly and effective start/finish routines – Use of voice, body language, movement around room – Use of praise – Prevention and management of inappropriate behaviour
Classroom climate – Secure and friendly environment where pupils feel confident in answering without fear of ridicule – Teachers model and encourage mutual respect – Pupils show good listening skills – Pupils enjoy the lesson – Pupils cooperate in pairs/groups	**Planning and differentiation** – Coherent short-term planning linked to prior and future learning – Appropriate level of challenge – Work well matched to full range of learners' needs (differentiation) – Effective use of classroom assistants

QUALITY ASSURANCE PROCEDURES – GUIDANCE FOR SUBJECT LEADERS

> Throughout their work, a subject leader ensures that practices improve the quality of education provided, meet the needs and aspirations of all pupils, and raise standards of achievement in the school.
>
> (National Standards for Subject Leaders)

The Quality Assurance file is a dynamic collection of documents, not an archive, which tells the on-going story of the subject area. It will help all teachers to have a developmental dialogue with their leader about standards of teaching and learning in their area, together with the actions needed to ensure continual improvement.

These procedures will promote high-quality leadership and provide evidence for self-evaluation which, in turn, will inform the Department Development Plan (DDP) and training needs.

The following provides a model for subject leaders to use, and covers the areas a subject leader will need to address in order to become fully self-evaluating and raise standards in the curriculum area:

1 Self-evaluation

Should be the result of discussion and reflection with the whole department, rather than the work of the HOD. Completed initially in September, then periodically updated. An updated SEF will be requested by SLT prior to any formal subject MER.

2 Department development plan (DDP)

Should be informed by the subject self-evaluation process, be owned by the whole department, and be closely linked to the Training Plan and School Development Plan.

- Assessment policy/procedures agreed within department.
- Work is sampled each half-term from each teacher in the subject area. The focus for the sampling (e.g. marking, literacy, homework) will be agreed in advance according to whole-school and/or departmental priorities.

QUALITY ASSURANCE PROCEDURES – GUIDANCE FOR
SUBJECT LEADERS *(continued)*

3 Scrutiny of pupil work

- Each Key Stage should be sampled twice over the course of
  the year.
- Formal feedback should be completed for each teacher and
  recorded in the QA file.
- Evidence from the sampling will inform modifications to the
  DDP.

4 Lesson observations

- Teachers should be observed during the course of the year
  by department/faculty leaders according to need. This can be
  delegated through faculties' line-management structures.
  Paired observations will ensure consistency.
- The focus of the observation may be specific.
- One observation will form part of the performance management process.
- The lesson observation process will also include consideration
  of the quality of planning.
- Documentation from the observations – particularly points for
  development – placed in QA file.
- Observations will inform training needs, may necessitate
  targets for improvement which should be revisited.

5 Department meetings

Department meeting should focus mainly on training and the
sharing of good practice, and this should be recorded in the QA
file.

6 Department CPD

An ongoing record of:

- Training needs (as identified by lesson observations/DDP
  priorities).
- Training undertaken and assessment of its impact, together
  with identification of future priorities.

**QUALITY ASSURANCE PROCEDURES – GUIDANCE FOR
SUBJECT LEADERS** *(continued)*

- Coaching.
- Peer observation.

7 Outcomes from data scrutiny

A record of actions undertaken in response to data:

- Response to exam results/data collections.
- Modifications to schemes of work following internal testing.
- Addressing issues of underachievement in particular groups (L2L (learn to learn), G&T, SEN, etc.), deployment of teaching assistants, etc.

8 Response to stakeholders

This section will contain the results of pupil and parent consultation (interviews/surveys/questionnaires) conducted to monitor development issues.

REFERENCES

Fullan, M. (1985) *The Meaning of Educational Change*, OISE Press

Hughes, M. (2003) *A Policy For Learning: a practical guide to writing or evaluating your teaching and learning policy*, Education Training and Support

Smith, A. (1996) *Accelerated Learning in the Classroom*, The School Effectiveness Series, Network Educational Press Ltd

Tizard, B. and Hughes, M. (1984) *Young Children Learning, Talking and Thinking at Home and at School*, Fontana

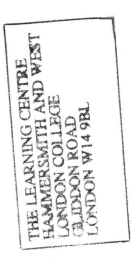